TASTEABLE

Publication Copyright © 2021, TasteTV / TCB-Cafe Publishing and Media LLC. All rights reserved
Above photo by Cirrus Aviation of the Vision Jet

TASTEABLE

1 EDITION
VOLUME 3

You are now reading Volume 3 of TASTEABLE Journal. This curated regular report is an experimental, limited edition, lifestyle publication that covers the best of Culture, Cuisine, Commerce, and Concepts.

SECTION: CONCEPTS & COMMERCE

Tasteful Finds: Your VIP Gift Bag	4
Your Next Porsche Will Be This Set Of Luxury Chefs Knives	5
Your Private Plane Has Arrived	6
Lindt Home Of Chocolate, Chocolate Museum, Switzerland	8
Sleek Timepieces For Your Wrist	10
The Need For Speed: The Emergence Of The New EV	12
The Industry Report	14
The Health Report	16
The Brand Report	18
The Wealth Report	19
Public Relations: Listen To Your Publicist's Advice	20
Innovator Profile: Click & Grow Smart Garden	22
Innovator Profile: Zavor Crunch Air Fryer	24

SECTION: LEADERS & TASTEMAKERS

Food, Fashion & Travel Media Stars Celebrate The TASTE AWARDS	29
TASTE HALL OF FAME: 8th & 9th Year Inductees	31
In Conversation With Chris Knight: CEO of Gusto TV	33
Fashion Media Closeup: Rocco Leo Gaglioti of FNL	38
Podcaster Closeup: Yorm Ackuaku	41
Travel Vlog Closeup: The Other Side Vlog	42
Lifestyle Celebrity Closeup: Michelle Harris of Alive & Well	44
Producer Closeup: Darley Newman	46
Style Influencer Closeup: Dandy Wellington	48
Culinary Icon Closeup: Diane Kochilas of My Greek Table	50
Recipe.TV Closeup: Lisa-Renee Ramirez	52
People To Know: Behind The Scenes At Red Carpet Events	55

SECTION: ART & DESIGN

TASTE PHOTO AWARDS: The Finalists	58
Musicians In The Spotlight: The Search For Inspiration	72
The Art Of Collecting Art	79
Collecting Art Books	80
Apple Store @ Apple Park: A Design Mecca For Tech Lovers	93
Report: Gear	98
Report: Eyewear	100

Style: Editors Choice	102
Perfumer Profile: Christi Meshell	120
Fragrance Guru: Sebastian Jara	122
Perfumer Profile: Olivia Larson	123
Scents: Editors Choice	125
Inspirations: A Lookbook of Rising Tastemakers	128

SECTION: FOOD & DRINK

Sitka Salmon Shares	135
RECIPE: Pork Wontons	139
RECIPE: Championships Chocolate Chip Cookies	140
RECIPE: Easy Rack Of Lamb	143
RECIPE: Dungeness Crab Cakes	144
RECIPE: Smoked Trout Potato Cake	146
RECIPE: Grilled Tajin & Maple Chicken Wings	147
RECIPE: Blueberry Cheesecake Ice Cream Bars	148
RECIPE: A Cake To Die For: Flourless Chocolate Cake	150
Looking For Natural Honey	151
RECIPE: Hot Ukrainian Borscht	152
Real Oyster Cult	154
RECIPE: Juicy Duck Breast In Red Wine Sauce	155
White & Dessert Wines: Editors Choice	157
Red Wines: Editors Choice	158
Collectors Report: Wine Travelers Gallery	160
Anaba Wines: John T. Sweazey and John Michael Sweazey	162
Broadside Wines: Anna Frizzell	163
Union Wine Company: Ryan Harms	164
Jerky & Snacks: Editors Choice	166
The Chocolate Report	168
Collecting Lifestyle Books	170
World Dog Surfing Championships Gift Guide	172

This Page: From the TATRAS Fall/Winter collection (shot at the iconic James Goldstein Residence, an architectural staple in Los Angeles)

TASTEABLE

Editor in chief: A.K. Crump

Photography: Credit and thanks goes to all acknolwedged photographers, as well as to all organizations and individuals that contributed photographs to this publication.

TCB-Cafe Publishing and media LLC
PO Box 471706
San Francisco, California 94147
www.TasteTV.com
USA

Copyright © 2021, TCB-Cafe Publishing and media / TasteTV
ISBN 978-0-9798640-2-5

All rights reserved. No part of this publication may be reproduced, stored in a retrieval system or transmitted in any form or by any means, electronic, mechanical, photocopying, recording or otherwise, without the prior permission of TCB-Cafe Publishing or the Author.

Every effort has been made to ensure the accuracy of the information in this book prior to publication. Neither TCB-Cafe Publishing or TasteTV, nor any of its employees or associates assume any legal liability or responsibility for the accuracy, completeness or usefulness of any information herein, or consequences arising from the use of this book or inclusion in it of photographs submitted by featured organizations, artists, businesses, or individuals. The publisher acts on good faith that photographs provided by featured organizations, artists, businesses, or individuals are authorized for use by the authors and by persons depicted in those photos, and is not liable.

www.TasteTV.com / www.CafePublisher.com

TASTEFUL FINDS: YOUR VIP GIFT BAG

It is well known that celebrities often receive free luxury goods and services, usually during an awards show or on the red carpet. This package of gifts is called a VIP Swag Bag. Fortunately you don't always have to be a celebrity or award winner to get one. In fact you can create one yourself with the exact same items. Here are some delicious selections for your own Personal Swag Bag. It includes luxury chocolates and confections, as well as other unique tastes from artisans such as Panache Chocolatier, CocoTutti, Toni's Toffee, DGZ Chocolates (Toffarazzi), Hazelnut Hill, Mel's Toffee, Luxx Chocolat, Regenie's, and Gowan's Heirloom Cider.

ABOVE: Toffarazzi Premium Toffee
BELOW: CocoTutti Chocolates, Raspberry Chocolate Bar

ABOVE: Truffles by Panache Chocolatier
BELOW: Mel's Toffee, Sea Salt Pretzel Toffee

ABOVE: Hazelnut Hill Salted Hazelnuts
BELOW: Regenie's Organic Nuts About Chips, Cranberry/Orange/Pecan

BELOW: Luxx Chocolat

YOUR NEXT PORSCHE WILL BE THIS SET OF LUXURY CHEFS KNIVES
The Porsche Design Chroma Type 301

A great chef needs great tools, and the same is true for home chefs as well. If you are the kind of person who likes the finer things in life, plus a very sharp edge, then take a look at these Porsche design knives.

Inspired by F.A. Porsche, the genius behind the iconic automobiles as well as the Porsche Design line of products, these Chroma Type 301 knives are fantastic for both professionals and serious home cooks. The razor sharp Japanese Chroma Type 301 comprises the entirety of the blade, while the handles are made of an entirely different material (18/10 stainless steel) to promote durability and ease of use. A pearl button is raised on both sides of the handle to the note the demarcation line between the two area, as well as to give tactile notice for where to hold the knife.

The tactile aspects of the knife rival the visual ones. Holding it in your hand is a very pleasant experience, not just because of its shape, but also because of the various metals used.

The blade requires a special Porsche sharpener so as to not dull or damage the edge. (pictured here is the Type 301 Design by F.A. Porsche 2 Knives Set P2 + P9, 7-inch Santoku + Paring Knife). In our experience, you are going to want to get the extra gear, because this knife is SHARP! Like, don't run it across your finger, use a piece of paper instead.

On many items in the Porsche Knife product line the handle is created with a unique wedge shape, which promotes firmer grips, greater balance, as well as the ability to display it in a way that generates envy and lust in everyone who sees it.

No, you should not have a knife just because people think it looks good. But if it works incredibly well, is super sharp, AND it looks good, then that's a win-win-win situation.

YOUR PRIVATE PLANE HAS ARRIVED
The Cirrus Vision Jet

If you just have $2 Million to spend, forget about getting your dream car. Think Bigger. Cirrus Aircraft has a new 6-seater personal jet that should take your 'bucket list' to an entirely new level…into the stratosphere.

Cirrus Aircraft has Vision Jet for you – the world's first single engine Personal Jet. The outside of the jet is recognizable on the tarmac from all others on the runway. The forked tail alone is enough to catch glances. Not to mention, the sexy and powerful single jet engine mounted on top of the fuselage.

The interior looks less like a plane and more like a luxury sedan. The seats are leather, as are some of the controls, and control dials don't look much different than what you would see driving on the road. If of course what you drove on the road could get you 1200 miles per tank.

Another benefit it that with this private jet you don't need a private pilot. If you are qualified, you can flight it yourself. No need to pre-schedule. No time-shares on planes. No major airports required.

A lot of what is at the pilot's seat is extremely user friendly, thanks to Garmin avionics major role in the plane's cockpit design. That design includes touchpad controls in some key areas.

The Vision Jet is the realization of a vision to re-imagine and reinvent the jet airplane in order to create a whole new category of aircraft —The Personal Jet. Simpler to fly and easier to operate and own, the Vision Jet is truly a revolution in personal transportation and the ONLY single-jet aircraft on the market. At a price point just under $2 million, and equipped with Cirrus' exclusive Cirrus Aircraft Parachute System (CAPS) (which set the aviation standard in aircraft safety) there's nothing like it available anywhere in the world.

LINDT HOME OF CHOCOLATE

CHOCOLATE MUSEUM, SWITZERLAND

Starting in 2020, the Lindt Chocolate Competence Foundation has invited small and large guests to take part in a journey of discovery into the wonderful world of chocolate. Planned and designed by ATELIER BRÜCKNER, the Lindt Chocolate Tour provides information on the origins, history and production of the mouth-watering delicacy, and involves all the senses in an exhibition area covering 1500 square metres.

The museum exhibition is located in the Lindt Home of Chocolate, a new building by Swiss architects Christ & Gantenbein at the headquarters of Lindt & Sprüngli in Kilchberg near Zurich. The world's highest, free-standing chocolate fountain in the foyer of the museum serves as the prelude to the world of chocolate. It is 9.30 metres high and circulates 1000 litres of liquid chocolate, flowing from a large, hovering wire whip down into a Lindor ball on the ground.

To start, visitors travel to a cocoa plantation in Ghana where they learn everything about the cultivation, harvesting, fermentation and drying of cocoa beans – as well as about the quality assurance process. How Switzerland became the "home of chocolate" is conveyed in the "Swiss Pioneers" room. The first chocolate factory was opened in Vevey as early as 1819. The all-round, hand-painted Swiss panorama is an invitation to make one's own discoveries.

The darkened adjacent room with the name "Chocolate Cosmos", which is surrounded by an atmospheric projection of stars, finally places chocolate as a product in a global context before visitors are taken to the "Chocolate Heaven" where they can taste a sample of Lindt products. Large-format Lindor balls supplement the narrative space. They are designed as photo booths.

Finally, the visitors cross a bridge over the foyer of the building to reach the "Innovation Lab", which opens out towards the light-filled interior. The exhibition architecture takes up the architecture of the building. The heart of the "Innovation Lab" is a real testing system, the entire interior of which can be seen. Specialists use this system to develop new chocolate creations. Augmented animation enables an X-ray view into the insides of the machines. The Chocolate Tour ends with a chocolate souvenir: A small bar of chocolate from the testing system, packaged in a golden ball, rolls through a lovingly designed marble run before it falls into the hands of the visitor.

SLEEK TIMEPIECES FOR YOUR WRIST
Vessel 24-Hour Automatic Watch

An elegant timepiece designed for everyday wear. The Vessel 24-Hour Automatic models offer subtle sophistication and thoughtful details in a classic silhouette. The dial features a 3-hand movement, a date window, and a 24-hour subdial. The etched crystal caseback gives a view into the automatic movement. Premium leather straps with soft suede baking guarantee a comfortable fit and long lasting durability. Quick-release pins on all our interchangeable straps allow you to easily switch up your look.

Materials:
- Stainless Steel Case
- Genuine Leather Strap with Leather Suede Backing
- Matte Black Dial
- Metal Watch Hands with LUM Fill

Features:
- 40mm Stainless Steel Case
- 20mm Strap Width
- Japanese Automatic 24 Hour Movement (21 Jewels)
- Screw-on Caseback with Inlaid Etched Crystal
- Waterproof up to 100m
- Quick-release straps
- Leather Keeper

Porsche Design Chronograph 911

Similar materials used on the 911 Porsche sportier are found on the Porsche Design Chronograph 911 GT3 watch. The dial is made of the same carbon found on parts of the car's chassis. The case is made of titanium and coated in black titanium carbide. The watch straps are made of the same leather and stitching thread used in the interior of Porsches 911 Speedster. The 'ignition lock' of the back of the Chronograph 911 Speedster is a winding rotor modeled on the 911 Speedster wheel.
www.porsche-design.com

Nomad Apple Watch Sport Band

Available in several new colors such as Black, Marine Blue, Dune, and Ash Green, the Nomad Sport Strap is great for the Apple Watch fan who leads an active lifestyle, from relaxing outdoors and workouts to much more rugged pursuits. Made of super resistant and ultra-durable fluoroelastomer (FKM rubber), the bands are fairly invulnerable to both physical and chemical wear and tear. In addition to being tough to damage, waterproof, and antimicrobial, the Sport Strap is also comfortable to wear. The Nomad design includes an inherent curve that gives the wrist enough airflow to breath, as well as venting ports that allow perspiration to dissipate. The Nomad Sport Strap is easy to install on your Apple Watch, and the attachment pins are made of strong, long-lasting aluminum. www.nomadgoods.com

THE NEED FOR *SPEED:*
THE EMERGENCE OF THE NEW EV

Electric vehicles, also known as EV's, are becoming more popular every year, especially in light of hastening climate change. In fact most major car manufacturers have an hour so by the 2130's they will be primarily electric vehicle focused. Of course everyone is aware that Tesla is a leader in this market, but there are other brands that are up-and-coming and making impressive gains. Two of those are Lucid and Polestar. They have expanded the number of vehicle showrooms located in high-end malls around the United States, and their performance statistics are definitely eye-catching.

LUCID
Year Founded: 2007
HQ: Newark, CA
Current EV: Lucid Air, Lucid Gravity
Range: 451-520 mi
Horsepower: 800 - 1111 hp
MPGe: 110-126 city / 111-125 highway
Dimensions: L 195.9" x W 76.3" x H 55.5"

POLESTAR
Year Founded: 1996 (by Volvo)
HQ: Gothenburg, Sweden
Current EV: Polestar Model 1, Model 2, Model 3
Range: 233-335 mi
Horsepower: 408 hp
MPGe: 96 city / 88 highway
Dimensions: L 181" x W 73" x H 58"

THE INDUSTRY REPORT

NENT's Nordic Media Network Expands

Nordic Entertainment Group (NENT Group), one of the world's fastest growing streaming groups, will launch its Viaplay streaming service in five new markets by the end of 2023. At launch, Viaplay's offering in the five new markets will comprise Nordic, local and international series, films, documentaries and kids content, both original and acquired. Viaplay will launch in the UK in the second half of 2022 and then in Canada, Germany, Austria and Switzerland during 2023. Viaplay will then be present in a total of 16 countries, compared with the original target of 15 announced in November 2020. NENT Group has also increased its target for the total number of Viaplay subscribers by the end of 2025 from approximately 10.5 million to approximately 12 million, of which approximately 6 million are now expected to come from international markets, compared with the original target of approximately 4.5 million.

NENT Group now expecting 2020-2025 compound annual organic sales growth in upper end of target ranges of approximately 18-20% for the Group and approximately 13-15% for the Nordic operations, with new target of approximately 23-25% compound annual organic sales growth for Viaplay in the Nordic markets. Anders Jensen, NENT Group President & CEO: "We have stepped up the pace and scale of Viaplay's international expansion. We have acquired virtually all of the international sports rights that we targeted and for multiple cycles in several cases; added one more market to our roll-out ambition; signed innovative partnership agreements; and raised the bar when it comes to our investments in original content. As a result, we are increasing our subscriber and revenue growth targets, as well as our target profitability levels. We are investing more short term to create even higher long term returns due to the considerable operating leverage that this creates. We are investing in this growth right now, in order to capitalize on the opportunity created as the shift to streaming video consumption continues to accelerate, and demand for high quality and locally relevant stories increases."

Photos Top: Anders Jensen, NENT Group President & CEO,
Bottom: Filippa Wallestam, EVP & Chief Content Officer

Lithuanian Film Tax Incentive

Vilnius, the capital of Lithuania, is rapidly becoming a crucial film production location in the region, favored by both local and international production companies. The main reasons for the attraction are the Lithuanian Film Tax Incentive and high-level professionals. The capital has also made global headlines when several large-scale projects shot in its streets during the past years: while Netflix's "Stranger Things" crew set up in the century-old Lukišk s Prison for Season 4, HBO chose the residential district Fabijonišk s for the cult-favorite miniseries "Chernobyl." Also, a Lithuanian feature film "Pilgrims" has just won the Orizzonti Award for Best Film at the 78th Venice Film Festival. Aside from world-class cinematic professionals, the Lithuanian Film Tax Incentive is one of the main appeals for foreign production companies. It enables feature films, TV series, documentaries to have 30% of filming costs reimbursed if they fulfill several main criteria: at least 80% of production costs must be incurred in the country, with the minimum spending amount of 43K. "Vilnius is fully prepared to accommodate the needs of foreign film crews, enable access to high-level professionals and a range of shooting locations, and facilitate the acquisition of filming permits," commented Pazikait . "Production teams come from the US and many of the largest European countries—Sweden, Norway, Finland, the United Kingdom, Germany, the Netherlands, to name a few. This year Vilnius and the rest of Lithuania were especially favored by the Scandinavian countries."

New Inductees into the National Inventors Hall of Fame

Seven innovation pioneers whose inventions range from cataract surgery to the modern automobile are being honored as part of the latest class of National Inventors Hall of Fame® (NIHF) Inductees, in partnership with the United States Patent and Trademark Office (USPTO). "As a nation, we innovate and we grow. Advancing innovation and entrepreneurship is critical to the future of our country, and the National Inventors Hall of Fame Inductees inspire a culture of invention," said Secretary of Commerce Gina M. Raimondo.

NEW INDUCTEES:

• Marian Croak: VoIP (Voice over Internet Protocol) Technology
Engineer Marian Croak has worked on advancing Voice over Internet Protocol (VoIP) technologies, converting voice data into digital signals that can be easily transmitted over the internet. Her work has allowed VoIP to become a practical reality by enabling reliability and high quality. Today, VoIP technology is vital for remote work and conferencing, as well as personal communications.

• Lonnie Johnson: Super Soaker
Engineer and entrepreneur Lonnie Johnson is the inventor of the Super Soaker®, which became a best-selling toy generating well over $1 billion in sales over its lifetime. Johnson's longtime research focuses on energy technology, and his work today includes advances in rechargeable battery technology and thermodynamic technology to convert thermal energy to electrical energy.

• Katalin Karikó and Dr. Drew Weissman: Modified mRNA Technology Used in COVID-19 Vaccines
Fundamental research by biochemist Katalin Karikó and immunologist Drew Weissman laid a critical piece of the foundation for the mRNA COVID-19 vaccines developed by Pfizer-BioNTech and Moderna. The mRNA vaccines have been crucial in the fight against the COVID-19 respiratory disease caused by SARS-CoV 2, a new coronavirus discovered in 2019. Nearly 1 billion mRNA vaccine doses have been administered worldwide since December 2020.

• Dr. Patricia Bath: Laserphaco Cataract Surgery (Posthumous)
Ophthalmologist Patricia Bath invented a new device and technique to remove cataracts known as laserphaco. Different than phacoemulsification that uses ultrasound, it could perform all steps of cataract removal, including making the surgical incision, destroying the lens and vacuuming out the fractured pieces.

• Carl Benz: Modern Automobile (Posthumous)
German engineer Carl Benz was the first to design a car around the internal combustion engine rather than adding an engine to an existing wagon or carriage, a critical insight in auto evolution. By integrating the engine, chassis and drive into a single entity, Benz set the standard for all future automotive design and engineering.

• James Buchanan Eads: American Infrastructure and Defense (Posthumous)
James Buchanan Eads created a series of inventions during the 1800s that improved transportation and the military defense of the Mississippi River region. His widespread innovations were crucial to river salvage, the success of the Union Navy during the Civil War, and infrastructure and engineering that enabled major advances in commerce.

Modern Life Increases Demand for "Peace of Life" Travel Insurance

Joe Cronin, President of International Citizens Insurance said: "People at a younger age are now seeking out travel insurance. There are more people in the 25-44 age group who are investing in travel insurance now than before the pandemic began, and the age group below that too, from age 18 up. And even though they understand their insurance premiums might be higher, there is a trend towards people opting for 'cancel for any reason' policies because they want to cover all the bases, whether they are deciding to move to a new country or to travel.

This type of coverage, also known as 'CFAR' insurance, is an excellent option for travel insurance buyers who worry they may have to cancel their journey for a reason that is not covered by trip cancellation coverage and want to recover at least a portion of their expenses. In a world emerging from a pandemic, this preference makes sense for many people."

A Science Amusement Park

WonderWorks bills itself as an amusement park for the mind, featuring a wide variety of "edu-tainment" opportunities. Each of the WonderWorks locations offers over 100 hands-on exhibits covering natural disasters and space discover, an imagination lab, a physical challenge zone, a far out gallery, and a light and sound zone. There are six WonderWorks locations, including Orlando, Myrtle Beach, Pigeon Forge, Panama City Beach, Syracuse, and Branson. Most are open every day of the year. For more information, visit the site at: https://www.wonderworksonline.com/.

Chicago Film & TV Production Studios

The City of Chicago continues to grow its presence as a location for film and television studios. This is due to the fact that there is a growing demand for film and television studios across the country, and that Chicago is centrally located with many public amenities and resources.

By some estimates the film industry in the Windy City creates over 20,000 jobs and has an economic value of over $750 million. Cinespace on the West Side is said to be one of the largest studios in North America. Others venues are being planned for the region. For example, the executive producer of the television series "The Chi," Derek Dudley, is joining with Loop Capital Chairman and CEO Jim Reynolds to bring another new studio to the metropolitan area. This venture is a $60 million project that will be called Regal Mile Studios, and has a projected scope of six sound studios and offices totaling about 220,000 ft.². Part of its base of operations will be near the historic Avalon regal theater on the city's South Side.

THE HEALTH REPORT

Walking Yourself to Better Health and Fitness

What is one of the most productive and effective ways of exercise? Walking!

Walking in fact is not just one of the most effective ways of exercise, it's also one of the oldest. Humans are designed to walk, it is how they evolved and thrived. It is how they overcame obstacles in the wild, found food and water, and expanded territory. You could say that in fact humans are literally meant to walk. So if this is true, it's clear what happens when you don't do what you're supposed to do. You are not as healthy, not as fit, and not as happy. This is exactly why walking is great for you.

Some of the benefits of walking include increased cardiovascular and pulmonary fitness for your heart and lungs. Walking also increases provides benefit, which is reducing the risk of heart disease and stroke. It also improves the management of chronic conditions such as hypertension and high cholesterol, as well as decreased joint and muscular pain, stiffness, and diabetes. Plus it can lead to stronger bones and better balance. Mentally, there is nothing more refreshing than taking a nice, calm, and refreshing walk to clear the cobwebs out of your mind, and getting good air into your lungs.

Most cities and states in North America and Europe have parks and hiking trails in which you can get out and walk. California has a lot of great spots where you can walk. In cities like San Francisco, it seems like everyone either walks or hikes on a regular basis. In Los Angeles, there are beautiful places along the boardwalk and the beaches where you can walk and walk and walk.

It is recommended that you walk at least 30 to 45 minutes nearly every day. You don't have to do it all at once, you can break it up into a 10 minute chunks, but the pace that you set is important. You don't need to break a sweat, but your goal is to get your heart pumping.

So get out there and take a walk, your body and your mind will thank you

Relax with These Tips and Tricks to Care for Your Plants

With more folks staying and working at home, a major trend in home and office décor is adding tropical plants and floral. It's an easy and affordable way to add color and style to any room, plus there are health benefits.

According to NASA, plants naturally filter the air of chemicals and other toxins linked to health problems, such as headaches and eye irritation.

Here are a few tips and tricks for success from the Hawaii Export Nursery Association, an organization representing Hawaii's plant and flower growers, for the exciting and exotic journey ahead:

　　Size doesn't matter. A small space sometimes demands a big statement plant. Don't be afraid to select oversized greenery that really commands a room.
　　Nature needs nurture. Remember these are living things. Just like a pet, you'll need to "feed" it daily with water. No better time to watch your indoor garden grow!
　　Not all plants are created equal. Plant origin is key. Plants and flowers grown in Hawaii not only give you that vacation vibe, they typically last longer.
　　Add instant style. A plant behind your desk or an orchid on your desktop will instantly stylize your web conferencing backdrop. Be prepared to say and share where you purchased your Dracaena Hilo Girl or Rhapis Excelsa Palm.

Tropical plants and floral are available at major box stores and retailers such as Home Depot, Lowe's, and Costco, or local nurseries and garden centers. If you are looking specifically for a Hawaiian-grown plants, look for the unique lava rock soil, which is a main differentiator and reason these plants thrive and grow so healthfully.

For more information on Hawaiian grown plants and flowers, visit HENA.org.

Organizing Your Home

Marty Basher, Home Design and Organization Expert for Modular Closets, has tips on organizing your home, especially in the kitchen. Says Marty, "In your freezer and pantry make sure you have what you need and that nothing is taking up space that is past its due date. There's no point freezing supplies if you can't find them later!

Other advice:
- Baskets in the freezer make it easier to store by type, so you know where to look for what you need.
- Put a list on the outside of the freezer to show what you have and how much of it you have. That way, when you go shopping, you'll know what you're low on at a glance.

Your pantry needs a good going over, to make sure you're well supplied in hot cocoa and tea, and perhaps less in pina colada mix! It's the perfect time to make sure that everything isn't past it's prime and needs to be thrown out.

https://www.modularclosets.com

Dealing with Trauma

Those struggling to move beyond a traumatic experience need to hear Dr. Randall Bell's empowering message: We all get knocked down. But with the right strategies, we can get back up, find our footing and grow in entirely new directions. In his latest book, "Post-Traumatic Thriving: The Art, Science, & Stories of Resilience," Dr. Bell provides clear, authoritative insights into what our options are in the aftermath of trauma and shares inspirational stories of real people who used the energy from their trauma to do something remarkable they wouldn't have done otherwise.

https://www.coreiq.com/books

Mental Health for Musicians

Songwriter and touring musician Brett Newski (who has played alongside the Pixies, Violent Femmes, Courtney Barnett, Manchester Orchestra, Better Than Ezra and more) has released his illustrated book, "It's Hard to be a Person: Defeating Anxiety, Surviving the World, and Having More Fun," accompanied by a soundtrack to the book featuring 8 original songs. The book has been endorsed by Stelth Ulvang of The Lumineers, "I love how easy Newski makes it to plow through the dark stuff with some well placed humor and grit." Newski been featured on Rolling Stone, NPR, American Songwriter, SiriusXM, Boston Globe, and Billboard. Newski presents three years' worth of drawings in his new book, "It's Hard to be a Person," offering mental health boosts through humor and relatable quips about the perils of living in our world with a mental illness. Newski's drawings offer a warmth and innocence that comforts readers and reflects their own experiences to assert that, despite the taboo of mental illness, most of us relate to each other on a deeper level when it comes to mental health.

https://brettnewski.com/.

Best Music to Listen to While Working from Home

Currently as much as 42 percent of the workforce is now or newly telecommuting full-time. This changing work pattern full of potential distractions can make the home office a challenging place for productivity. According to Rent.com, the right music can help you be more productive, more creative, or just happier. A silent room can be just as distracting as an over-stimulated environment. It can also drown out the sounds of your partner working in the other room, a cranky baby, a needy puppy, noisy neighbors, or the sounds of the city. What is the best kind of music to listen to? Genres such as classical, instrumental, or feel-good music can be the difference between a productive or not-so-productive day.

5 Reasons to Add Quinoa to Your Diet

Cookbook author Catherine Gill, creator of "The Complete Quinoa Cookbook," gives five stand out healthy reasons why people should give quinoa a try and consider it part of your regular meal planning.

1. Quinoa is a Perfect Protein: There aren't many food items out there that are considered a whole or "perfect" protein. What that means is that it is considered a complete protein, containing all of the nine essential amino acids that our bodies need, but cannot make on their own.

2. Quinoa is a Superfood: Speaking of being super, this ancient grain is also considered to be a superfood as well. The reason for this classification is easy: quinoa is jam packed with not just protein, but it is high in fiber and also contains lots of vitamins and minerals. It also has impressive amounts of magnesium, B-vitamins, potassium, iron, phosphorus, calcium, vitamin E, amongst others.

3. Quinoa is Low on the Glycemic Index: Since quinoa is a low glycemic index food, meaning your body uses its energy slowly and over time, it is recommended for people who seek diets which are lower in carbs or are looking for foods to add to a diet in order to lose weight and improve health. Some individuals who suffer from Type-2 diabetes, for example, are often advised by their physicians to consume less carbs and add low glycemic choices to their daily diets.

4. Quinoa is Gluten-Free: Quinoa is one of the grain-like seeds that many people think is a carbohydrate type of food like rice, but the key difference is that it is totally free of gluten. Many people have allergies to gluten or suffer from illnesses such as celiac disease which increases their need for alternate "grains" to eat. And for example, for some who previously enjoyed wheat-based cereals, they can simply grab cereal that's made with quinoa.

5. Quinoa Contains Important Plant Flavonoids: Flavonoids are plant compounds, or are otherwise known as antioxidants, which have been shown to offer people with many health benefits including anti-inflammatory, anti-viral and even anti-cancer effects. Experts who study nutrients and flavonoids in foods have discovered high levels of two very vital flavonoids called quercetin and kaempferol are in quinoa. The antioxidant quercetin is so high in quinoa that it has more of the antioxidant quercetin that even cranberries do!

www.hatherleighpress.com

THE BRAND REPORT

PortoVino Wine Purse

Stylish yet discreet, perfect for carrying around wine safely and comfortably. The creators designed it with fashion in mind, so you will look and feel great taking the bag to any social setting. The PortoVino Wine Purse is environmentally friendly, and made of vegan leather and lined with a soft cotton interior and a hidden, insulated compartment. It can hold up to up to 2 bottles of wine or other beverages. Not just for wine, it also holds up to 2 full party pouches AND all your essentials in a separate compartment. For more discretion in your wine country trips (or to the cinema), the purse has a designer flap on the back hides the pouring spouts until you are ready to use it. If you're thinking less about wine, it additional can be used for beer, mixed drinks, water or even juice for friends and family.

https://porto-vino.com/

Premium Sake Brand SOTO includes Top Tennis Player as Investor Tennis Star Naomi Osaka

Japanese sake, one of the fastest growing alcohol categories in North America over the last decade, is expected to expand by a further 51% in the next year. One prominent beneficiary of this consumer trend: SOTO Sake, an award-winning, premium Japanese sake brand produced in Niigata, Japan is sold in thousands of locations in the U.S., Canada, and Europe. Naomi Osaka has been named as an investor and creative consultant to the SOTO brand. "Naomi's elegant, serene demeanor and philosophical outlook on her life and young career are big reasons we wanted her to be involved with SOTO," says Billy Melnyk, who co-founded the brand with business partner Dan Rubinoff. "Appreciating true Japanese sake is a transportive and enlightening experience, and we wanted our first publicly celebrated investor to embody that." In her role as a creative consultant to SOTO, Osaka (who was coincidentally born in Osaka, Japan) will lend her generational and cultural insights to the brand as it grows and promotes itself, with proper responsibility, to a new generation of social drinkers. SOTO intends to use Naomi's emotional and cultural intelligence, and her growing status as a role model for women of all ages and races, to introduce historic elements of Japanese culture and craftsmanship to millions of people around the world through the brand's marketing and the experience of enjoying Japanese sake. "As a native of Japan, I am proud to be involved with a product that is authentically Japanese, said Naomi Osaka. "SOTO's status as a made-in-Japan, traditional 'Japanese sake' is another major reason I'm supporting the brand.

www.sotosake.com

Nicki Minaj Launches Canned Wines

Nicki Minaj's Myx Fusion Beverages has released a line of lower-calorie and low alcohol canned wines. The first is the MYX Light Chardonnay, along with the MYX Light Rosé. "The MYX Fusions team worked hard with the winemaker to produce these amazing wines. These wines represent a milestone in winemaking, using age-old methods of early harvest and creative innovation," says Peter D. Reaske, MYX Beverage LLC CEO. "We knew if we entered the on-fire 'light' category, we needed a product that didn't compromise taste or quality, and at 75 calories per serving, MYX Light delivers exactly what consumers are looking for – great-tasting, 'sessionable,' refreshing, easy-to-drink, lower-calorie wines."

THE WEALTH REPORT

Citizenship Investment Market Shows Strong Growth from Covid Pandemic

Demand for investment driven residency and citizenship has shown strong growth over the last seven years with the market for inward investment into government programs now estimated at over $20 billion worldwide. New enquiries in the 12 months to March 2021 rose 12.3% while sales increased 43.9% over the corresponding period. La Vida has seen a significant rise in enquiries since the onset of the pandemic but critically those enquiries are of a far more serious nature resulting in clients proceeding with their plans according to La Vida CEO Paul Williams. "We're seeing far greater urgency from clients now who perhaps were previously hesitant or even not in the market at all for our services. Clients are saying "never again do we want to be exposed in that way whatever the next crisis brings". It's as if everyone just wants to move on and second citizenship and passports are a key part of their Plan B preparation despite the current travel restrictions."
www.goldenvisas.com

Vinfolio Fine Wine Investment Report

Vinfolio, one of the country's leading fine wine companies, recently released a comprehensive Fine Wine Investment Report outlining the current state of global wine market investments. Over the last three decades investment-grade fine wine has performed very strongly against most major asset classes. Furthermore, wine has a pleasingly low correlation with other assets during periods of market disruption—making it a valuable support to a diversified portfolio.

Highlights from the Fine Wine Investment Report include:

1) VinPulse Current Market Overview - Bypassing pandemic-related difficulties, many fine wine segments like Italian and Bordeaux wines have soared over the last year and a half.
2) Vinfolio Top 10 - The hottest wines on the market right now, based on growth statistics.
3) Regions to Watch - Invest in Bordeaux, Burgundy, Champagne, Rhône, Italian, and U.S. wines. Vinfolio explores what to look for and stay away from in each segment.
4) Expand Your Collection - Wine to Buy Now: 2018 Tenuta San Guido Sassicaia, Fine Australian Wine, McLaren Vale's Clarendon Hills

Real Estate Investing in Costa Rica

Michael Krieg with United Country Real Estate | International Luxury Properties shares some details and tips regarding real estate transactions so you can wisely invest in Costa Rica. Many of the details to complete a transaction in Costa Rica look very similar; one of the biggest challenges is time. Time moves slowly in Costa Rica. Contact Michael to learn more about the process and start your search for the property that will suit your lifestyle in Costa Rica. Two of them are that you should find a property you love in an area that suits your lifestyle, and understand that pricing is always a plus or minus since "comparables" aren't as common in these markets. Also, It is recommended that a Costa Rican corporation is created and that such corporation is the owner of the property vs. you as the individual. This provides several advantages, especially when it comes to any liability.

Secrets to Financial Independence

Author David Parker says, "Most people in this country don't realize they are living way beyond their means," Parker says. The prescription he suggests for wealth creation may not be easy — but it is certainly effective. He urges all young people, regardless of their earning power, to invest half their annual income. "Even those not especially creative or brilliant," he says, "will generate significant income from their investments within 10 years." Parker shares the perspectives and principles on which he also built successful careers as an entrepreneur and investor in INCOME AND WEALTH: David Parker Essays — Volume One. The lessons that Parker shares with readers in this thought-provoking, transformational work encapsulate the author's 40-year study of economic history and principles. www.davidparkeressays.com

How Stock Splits Work for Investors

A stock split happens when a company decides that its price per share for the stock is too high for small investors to afford. For example, it's easy for an investor to buy stock that is valued at $10 or $50 a share, but it is much harder for them to purchase a stock that is valued at $1,500 or $3,000 a share. They may not be able to afford even one share, whereas they can afford several if the price is much lower. The split therefore makes the stock market much more fair to small investors, and those who are not backed by giant mutual funds, family trust offices, or investment companies. When a stock split happens, the company announces that for each share of stock you currently own, after a certain date you will then get more shares for each share that you already have. You may get two for the price of one, or you may get five for one. It all depends on the company. But if the price was at $1,500 a share and it splits to 2 for 1, then each price is now $750 a share. You still have the same amount of money invested, $1500, but now you own twice as many shares. This is why we say that theoretically it should not matter if the stock splits or not. Your investment amount should not change. Historically however what happens is that for exciting or fast-moving stocks, especially tech stocks, what you see is that when the price drops to a more affordable level for smaller investors, they in turn buy more of it, and therefore increase the demand and subsequent price of that share. Does this mean that you should jump on board when a stock announces a stock split? Possibly, but possibly not. If you were already going to purchase the stock then you should go ahead. But if you think just jumping on board before the stock split will get you extra returns, then that is basically a risky investment. The stock's future value really depends on the performance of the company itself.

PUBLIC RELATIONS:
LISTEN TO YOUR PUBLICIST'S ADVICE

Public Relations often seems like a soft art, where it is assumed that all you need to do is wear nice clothes, go to fashionable parties, call reporters on the phone, or write a catchy press release. Or just live like they do on the television series "Gossip Girl." The truth is far from that, PR takes a lot of time and work to get the best story in front of the right outlet. After that, you still have to get and keep their attention, and manage the ongoing relationship.

There are tons of failures with each effort, and clients do not always appreciate what has to happen to make things work, so the satisfaction of any success is that much greater.

We've talked with several outstanding publicists and asked them one importan question:

WHAT IS SOME OF THE BEST ADVICE YOU GIVE TO YOUR CLIENTS?

•

"Respond in a timely manner to media requests"

"Provide media as much lead time for time-sensitive matters, events."

Vicki Jakubovic
VICKIGJPR
West Orange, NJ

"All marketing is visual marketing. Make sure you've got sensational photos and videos of what you want to promote. Do not skimp on the quality of your visual assets."

"If you can't organize it, you can't execute it. Planning time is imperative and valuable time to each promotion. Make sure you give each project enough planning and ramp up time to be able to fully excel in your execution."

Margot Black
Founder/Director
BlackInkPR.com

"Your agency is your partner. It is a two way street in terms of give and take. The more you collaborate, inform and involve them along the strategic path, the richer the outcome will be for all."

"A great relationship with a marketing/PR partner is like a marriage. The more you communicate and support each other through both challenging and good times, the deeper the experience will be. Some clients focus on the 'what have you done for me lately' instead of realizing that marketing is a series of short, medium and long term wins. Be in it for the long haul and you will be rewarded. Value and appreciate each other and don't forget to always include the personal, human touch. Empathy is the key to success."

Kimberly Noelle Charles, DipWSET
President and Founder
Charles Communications Associates

"The best advice for brands is to understand how to enhance and expand their visibility and messaging. In a larger sense however, a great way to grow your brand is for it to be purpose-driven. Make a product, a service, or a brand that benefits the world in some way. Having a larger reason culminates in consumers looking forward to not only enjoying your product, but enjoying being a part of a greater good.A major importance is for brands to understand how to increase their visibility. Along with having an amazing product and potentially a great for-good component to their brand, expanding your visibility to a larger and broader audience will significantly increase the potential consumers you will have. With visibility, people across the nation have the opportunity to learn about you, your products, and the company you worked so hard to build.In addition, messaging is essential to any brand. Understanding what makes you different from all of your competitors can give you the edge in the market. Whether it is producing healthier products, using better ingredients, creating things in a more sustainable way, understanding the best ways to message this is necessary for a growing brand. With messaging you are able to grow the trust and credibility any successful brand requires."

Heather DeSantis
CEO
Publicity For Good

PR is really just people relations and understanding how to tell an engaging story. A good PR person, team or agency will know intuitively how to best sell your brand to the media and the general public. Trust in your PR team to guide the process."

Heather Noll
President
Chalkboard Communication

"Respond in a timely manner to media requests"

"If you can't organize it, you can't execute it."

"The more you collaborate, inform and involve them along the strategic path, the richer the outcome will be for all."

"Along with having an amazing product and potentially a great for-good component to their brand, expanding your visibility to a larger and broader audience will significantly increase the potential consumers you will have."

INNOVATOR PROFILE

CLICK & GROW SMART GARDEN

End the days of trying to grow limpy, pale herbs and vegetables on your windowsill with the Click and Grow Smart Garden. Finally an indoor garden kit that looks good and works well, especially for those who want to grow more than 1 crop over the entire year.

Originally inspired by NASA's attempts to grow fresh food in space, other cool Smart Garden features include:

   A wide selection of pre-seeded plant capsules with over 40 types of fresh herbs and fruits
   Grow everything you eat pesticide-free.
   The Smart Garden soil uses patented nano-tech growth medium that accelerates the plant growth without jeopardizing quality
   Can be used in kitchen, living room, office or lobby

Side benefit, the built-in LED grow light might just help you knock off any of those blues from being indoors too much.

We've been crushing on our Click and Grow Smart Garden for over two years, and for good reason. It is the perfect way to grow herbs and flowers indoors under any conditions. You just set it up, plug it in, and use a pre-made seed pod. Add water, set the light timer. Done. That's it. Just sit back and watch the plants grow. And grow they do. Our Basil and Mint both went a bit nuts, we couldn't pick them fast enough.

What has placed the Click and Grow Smart Garden back on our Must-Have Gift list is that they continue to expanded sizes, and more importantly, have a larger variety of plants. Fragrant Rosemary is one, as is Mibuna. Also, for those who want to "experiment," you can use an empty "Experimental" soil pod and add your own seeds of whatever herb strikes your fancy.

INNOVATOR PROFILE

ZAVOR CRUNCH AIR FRYER

We have tested several different air fryers, and some are great, and some are not so great. One of the ones that we think is really nice is the Zavor Crunch Air Fryer Oven. It is perfect not just for amateurs who are just getting started with air fryers, before also for experts who use them all the time. One thing in particular that we really love about this item is that it gives you two racks to cook on at the same time, and has a capacity of 12.7 quarts. This doubles the amount of food that you can prepare, as well as doubles the types of food that you can cook simultaneously.

The Zavor Crunch Air Fryer Oven controls are intuitive and easy to use. It's a very simple 1-2-3 step approach. First step is plugging it in the appliance and turning it on. After that you just set the TEMP and TIME, and you're pretty much done. Or you can use one of the blue LED display buttons that show different types of foods or food groups such as Fries, Meat, Seafood, Pizza, Vegetables, Bake and Dehydrate, and then automatically set the temperature and cooking time with them. We have found that those buttons are useful, but it is much more useful to have a written guide that will say for a particular type or food or vegetable the specific temperature and length. Fortunately in the instruction booklet that comes with the Zavor there is such a written guide. There are also written Time & Temp guides for air frying that are available online.

Most air fryers require usually a bit of olive oil or another oil on the item to be cooked. This is done simply by putting them in a bowl and a bit of olive oil, then lightly tossing, then adding the food to the rack of the air fryer. The Zavor Crunch Air Fryer Oven has a non-stick drip pan at the bottom to catch drips and for easy cleaning.

We tested different types of recipes in the Zavor Crunch Air Fryer Oven over a period of several weeks. Everyone loves crispy tofu, so of course we tried it with crispy tofu in a sesame sauce. It worked perfectly. Of course french fries are the most popular recipe for air fryers, so we tested the Zavor with different types of potatoes to see what differences there might be in the fries. In addition we tested different sizes and cuts of fries. Regardless of the type or cut, the fries came out very tasty. Our team had a difficult time not eating them all in one go. Yet another addiction.

We also tried air frying Brussel Sprouts to see if they would become crispy. They did, although we still think that roasted in the oven is probably the best place for the tastiest outcome.

In the Zavor Crunch Air Fryer Oven we tried cooking fried chicken, which came out very well, and this was a surprise because one of the biggest fails people have with air frying is when they decide to fry chicken in them. It really takes a very specific combination of ingredients, coating, and temperature to get what most people would want in their fried chicken. This includes having the breading staying on the chicken and not sliding off. The Zavor fortunately came through this ultimate challenge with flying colors.

Cleanup with the Zavor is easy, as most components inside are removable and non-stick, for easy hand washing. Another useful feature that the Zavor Crunch Air Fryer Oven has is the option to create rotisserie chicken. An attractive option without a doubt, no doubt related to its larger capacity as well as ability to hold a custom spit. We hope to test this feature at a future date.

Our biggest success with the Zavor Crunch Air Fryer Oven was actually with carrot fries. This recipe calls for you to take small baby carrots and cut them in half, then coating them with olive oil lightly, as well as spices, and then adding them to the air fryer. They come out just as delicious as potato-based french fries, but of course are less starchy and more healthy.

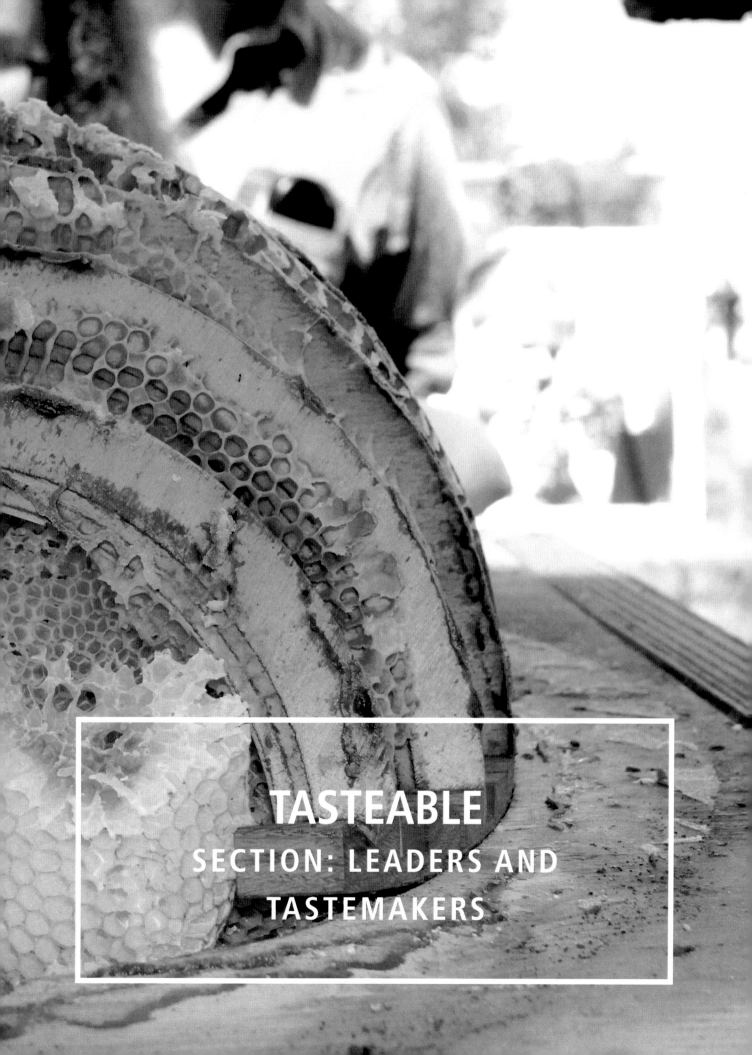

TASTEABLE
SECTION: LEADERS AND TASTEMAKERS

ANDREW ZIMMERN
HOST, PRODUCER

Cooking with Cal
NBC's Today Show
BREAKOUT FOODIES OF THE YEAR AWARD

TIE

New-Soul Kitchen with Chef Jernard

Elba vs. Block

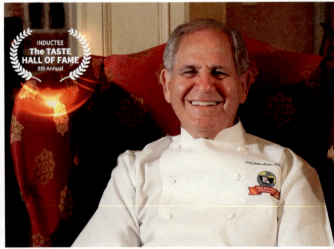

FOOD, FASHION & TRAVEL MEDIA STARS CELEBRATE THE TASTE AWARDS

The Annual TASTE AWARDS announced the Award Winners as well as various Special Achievement Award Winners (Honorees) for the recent awards show. Many are well known celebrities, but there were plenty of rising stars and new names. The TASTE AWARDS spotlight the year's best achievements in food, fashion, and home lifestyle programs on television, in film, and on the web. Taking place in Los Angeles, they are the premier awards celebrating the year's best in Food, Fashion, and Lifestyle programs on Television, in Film, in Streaming & Online Video, in Apps, and in Podcasts and on Radio. The Annual Awards has included appearances by stars, celebrities, producers and executives from networks and platforms such as the Food Network, the Style Network, Bravo, the Neflix, Amazon Prime, TLC, Discovery, Lifetime, E! Entertainment Television, PBS, NBC, ABC, the CW, HGTV, the Travel Channel, YouTube, Hulu, YouTube, Vimeo, Vice, LiveWell Network, Esquire Network, Bio/FYI Channel, iHeart Radio, HBO, MyxTV, Small Screen Network, StyleHaul, PTA, Zagat, Mode Media, WatchMojo, Amazon Prime, Netflix, Lifetime Network, Vox Media, and more. www.TheTasteAwards.com

THIS PAGE:

Ming Tsai with Andrew Zimmern

Selena Gomez in Selena + Chef (HBO Max)

OPPOSITE PAGE:

Andrew Zimmern

Today Show's Dylan Dreyer in Cooking with Cal (NBC)

Chef Jernard Wells (Cleo TV)

Idris Elba in Idris vs Block (Roku)

Chef John Folse (LPB/PBS)

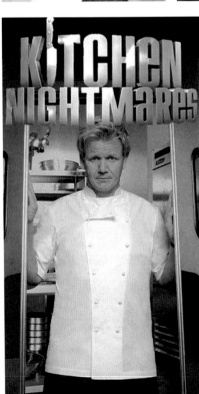

Images courtesy of Inductees, Production Stills and Publicists.

TASTE HALL OF FAME

8TH & 9TH YEAR INDUCTEES

Recently the TASTE AWARDS Committee, organizers of the Annual TASTE AWARDS celebrating the year's best in food, fashion and lifestyle programs on television, in film, online and on radio, announced the inductees into the eighth and ninth classs of the TASTE Hall of Fame.

Each year Inductees are selected based on either having received numerous TASTE AWARDS and finalist nominations over the years, or having made a significant impact in the world of taste and broadcast entertainment.
www.TasteHallOfFame.com

8TH HALL OF FAME INDUCTEES

- A Taste of Louisiana
- Andre Leon Talley
- Architectural Digest
- Buddy Valastro
- Burt Wolfe
- Chefs Table
- Debi Mazar & Gabriele Corcos
- Dining with the Chef
- Dwell
- Engineer Your Space
- Equitrekking
- Gail Simmons
- Gary Vaynerchuk
- Hotel Impossible
- House Hunters International
- House of Style (CNN)
- How Do I Look? (Style Network)
- James Charles
- Jon Taffer
- Kitchen Nightmares
- Lucky Chow
- Masterchef Latino
- Michelle Bernstein
- Nigella Lawson
- Paint this with Jerry Yarnell
- Questlove
- Real Housewives of Beverly Hills
- Ruth Reichl
- Unwrapped
- WatchMojo
- Wine Road Podcast
- Zendaya

9TH HALL OF FAME INDUCTEES

- Aarón Sanchez
- AMC Networks international - Latin America
- Andre 3000
- Animal Planet
- Binging with Babish
- Bob Ross
- Bon Appétit
- British GQ
- Chip and Joanna Gaines
- Cooks Country
- Cool Japan
- Curtis Stone
- Daniel Boulud
- Elsa Klensch
- Francis Ford Coppola
- French Guy Cooking
- Garden Smart TV
- Guy Fieri
- Hell's Kitchen
- Hot Ones
- Hubert Keller
- Kylie Kwong
- Ludo Lefebvre
- Mary Berry
- Million Dollar Listing
- Outside TV
- Pati Jinich
- Powerhouse Productions
- Stacy London
- Stanley Tucci
- The Property Brothers
- The Victory Garden
- Tim Gunn
- Today Food
- Tom Douglas

IN CONVERSATION WITH CHRIS KNIGHT:
CEO of Gusto TV & Gusto Worldwide

Margaret McSweeney, Kitchen Chat: What is Gusto TV? Can you share with us the background? We saw that great clip but what a visionary you are to see this need in the marketplace.

Chris Knight, Gusto Worldwide: Gusto TV, as we like to say is the world's best food channel. We launched originally here in Canada as a linear pay television channel as an alternative to what was in the market and the thinking being that when you went home at night, there were lots of different channels for sports and movies and dramas but really only one place to go that consistently had food programming. And we felt that there was room for an alternative to that. And we launched the channel and it's been wildly successful and growing by leaps and bounds ever since. We're now on, as well as in Canada we're in the UK. We're about to launch in a couple places in the EU. We're in Singapore, China, Australia, the US of course, Latin America. And we continue to grow.

Chef Jaime Laurita, Kitchen Chat: That is amazing. So as you're building this incredible empire, what is your next big goal?

Chris Knight: Well, the next big goal I guess, our goal is to continue to launch in new markets and new territories. So we established the foothold in Asia, for instance, in Singapore, and then with China Mobile in China and also with SBS in Australia. But we've just dipped our toe in the Asian market. We haven't done anything in Middle East or Africa yet. So those are tremendous opportunities for us. And really we've just established ourselves in the US. We've been on really with you guys for about a year and a half, so we're established in the US. Now it's our goal to grow the business, more eyeballs, as we say in the business.

Jaime Laurita: Nice.

Margaret McSweeney: Fantastic. And what are some of the biggest challenges that you're facing right now, of course in addition to COVID restrictions?

Chris Knight: Well the biggest challenges for any business is discoverability, regardless of the business that you're in. Are competitors are large multi-billion dollar corporations who spend more on fridge magnets than our entire marketing budget. So discoverability for any business is the

biggest challenge. Ongoing fun challenge is constantly finding new talent, new talent who bring different perspectives, new voices, fresh attitudes, and have new stories to tell because we're all about telling stories.

Jaime Laurita: That's amazing. What other interesting opportunities do you think are coming? Tell me about some interesting opportunities that you think are on the forefront.

Chris Knight: Yeah. So when you're trying to grow an international brand, right? So I think what makes us different for instance say than when you look at our competitors, a 100% of what you see on Gusto is produced by us. So there's no acquired programming from anybody else. So we set out to build Gusto or in Latin America and France its Gusto or Gusto. We chose the name Gusto because it translates into so many different languages and cultures.

Chris Knight: Right now if you take a look at our programming schedule… I was doing some quick math. We feature more than 40 different cultures and 40 different cuisines from Vietnamese to Venezuelan, from Kenyan to Sri Lankan, Norwegian and of course the staples, Italian, French, Greek. And so we built Gusto.

We say food is the one true global language and Gusto speaks all dialects.

Jaime Laurita: Wow.

Margaret McSweeney: Wow.

Chris Knight: So we're very inclusive, very multicultural. We explore culture, we celebrate through food and that's really our goal is to make emotional connections and celebrate through food. And celebrate the things that make us different but also at the same time reminding us of the things that we share in common and eating some good food along the way.

Margaret McSweeney: I love that. You truly are setting the global table for all of the viewers. So each year, Chris, you launch new Gusto series. So how do you decide which series to green light? How do you produce them? And as far as talent, how do you decide upon that, location etc.? What are some of the components of your decision making that go into that?

Chris Knight: Well, as executive producer and president of Gusto, my main job is to torture everyone who works here and try and

figure out what we're going to do next. We're in a very fortunate place in that, as I told you, we produce everything ourselves. As you can see on the wall behind me there's names of a whole bunch of shows and they move up and down the rotation. We're constantly changing. We just finished a show called Combination Plates and we're about to shoot a new series called "Some Assembly Required." And then that'll take us to Christmas. And then next year there's four or five different series that we're trying to decide which one to do next. Now, of course right now with COVID, that restricts our shooting. So we have this really great show we do called DNA Dinners that requires multiple crews and multiple locations with lots of people coming in, out of homes and restaurants.

Chris Knight: And so programs like that. And another great documentary series we do called Great To Plate. Those sort of programs we've had to shelve until we are a 100% sure that everybody who works with us is going to be safe. So for the time being, our plans were right now that we would be shooting in Denver, LA, Singapore, Mexico City. Because we send people there, because we produce our own content we send people all over the world. So that changes what and how we're making programming. Now, fortunately right over there about 30 yards that way is our own state of the art studio. So we're back in production. We've been back in production since June because we have a secure facility.

Chris Knight: Everything at Gusto is done by Gusto. So we do all of our own post production, our music, our graphics, recipe testing. We have a 1000 sq. Ft. kitchen with full-time chefs, full-time writers who are also chefs and everything is produced by us. So currently we're producing studio based programming until this madness has receded. And how we choose programs? It evolves and changes constantly. What we're looking for from our hosts are people who can make emotional connections. I've been doing this for over 20 years and worked with hundreds of different hosts. And the thing about, of course, when you're doing food programming is, more often than not the talent that ends up in front of the camera are not trained actors. They are

chefs or they come from the other side of the business, right?

Jaime Laurita: Right.

Chris Knight: And so we have to work with them and nurture them and give them all the opportunity to grow and make that emotional connection through the camera. But because viewers are so sophisticated now and they have so many choices, talent does not have the opportunity to grow into the job. You got to kill it out of the gate. If you go back and you look at Jamie Oliver's first show The Naked Chef, all those years ago, the guy mumbled and stumbled, wouldn't look at the camera. You could hear the producer off to the side, lobbing him questions. But he clearly had something in him. But he could grow into it, right? No, not anymore. We work very closely with our talent. Because we have so many different cultures on Gusto we have talent from all over the world. And so we have a full time people who just start constantly looking for people that we can work with.

Jaime Laurita: That was a great answer. I'm getting chills.

FASHION MEDIA CLOSEUP:
Rocco Leo Gaglioti of FNL

Model, actor, director, producer, and more, Rocco Gaglioti is well-known for being the very first person to put fashion content online through the creation of Fashion News Live.

Where are you based now? Los Angeles, Las Vegas and a secret place in Europe

Why? Running a network with 28 channels keeps me very busy and I work with my teams from all over the world.

What is your Favorite Vacation Spot? The Greek Islands with the crystal clear water that I love to jump in and swim.

What is Your Favorite Item of Clothing or Designer? I love a nice suit jacket

What is your passion? To creative. I love to come up with an idea and make it happen with a team.

What was the inspiration for FNL? Icons of the industry were very influential and inspirational to me, encouraging the creation of exclusive and unique content within this network. The FNL Network is an American television network that not only creates content for a large-scale audience but also was my moment to make my mark in this world.

How did you come up with the name? FNL Network stands for "Fashion", "News", and "Lifestyle"--all of which are encompassed within the channel.

What do you love about it? FNL Network offers a combination and wide variety of content with fashion, film, travel, beauty, health, and reality TV all within the channel. There was a need for inclusivity and diversity in a fashion that was a major inspiration during the construction of the network, and the network brought this inclusivity to life.

What is the most challenging part? This project was built from the ground up. It was a tremendous feat, but it thrives. "Although creating the network was and still is hard work, when you love your job it never really feels like work. Inspiration challenges your creativity and pushes people like me and my team to create content that our audience hasn't seen before. The bottom line is I love what I do, and I will put everything I have into it."

How did you go about getting involved or even starting this endeavor from a business or professional standpoint? The network, from the start, has had a consistent and loyal audience thanks to the channel's variety. It has a diverse show lineup including the following: Beauty Tips, Courtney, featuring Courtney Stodden, Carol Alt's Living Room, City Showcase, Fashion News Live, Film Corner, The FNL Network Talkshow, FNL Vintage, Model Diaries, and Street Style and much more.

What kind of trends are you seeing now in this space? International Digital Fashion Week was created out of a need for an accessible digital fashion week. The idea came about as fashion week events worldwide were canceled due to the Covid-19 virus. IDFW aims to provide a platform for designers around the world to be able to showcase their work to a larger audience, even in instances like the pandemic. This can be streamed only on FNL Network.

Anything you wish you had known in this industry when you first started? Great question. Well I started in this industry when I was about 13 years old. I had no idea about anything and each step has been a huge learning experience. I wish I had a manager that could have guided me as young talent and shown me the ropes. I was like a little kid that jumped into a pool full of sharks and had to learn how to fight them off and swim away.

Any tips for those aspiring to do better in this media space? Be Original, be yourself—follow your instinct and don't conform to other people's expectations. Don't wait for an opportunity to come to you, create your own. If you are knocking and the door doesn't open. Do not give up! Just make your own door and open it. Take a look at what's already been done, how it was successful, and how you could make it better, then develop your own flair. And once you start, never give up!

How much do you use Social Media as part of the business or project? Social Media outlets are utilized regularly to keep our audience up-to-date on the latest information and releases.

How do you get your ideas for the project? Often they pop in my mind when I am relaxing. I do not even try. It has always been like that for me.

Who is doing work in this space that you really admire? Netflix is who I admire. I love that many press outlets and people have called FNL Network the Netflix of the fashion and lifestyle world **Do you find that people recognize you on the street?** Yes, it is very nice at times.. Sometimes I do not want to be bothered but I am always kind with everyone. We have to appreciate our fans because we are who we are because of them.

What's next for You and this Project? We will continue building the network and continue making it available on multiple platforms around the world for free. We are currently available on all Apple devices, Android devices, Google Play Store, HUAWEI AppGallery, Roku TV, Amazon Fire TV, Android TV, Samsung and LG TVs.

We are constantly growing and creating new content all the time and working with contact providers to create an amazing experience for all of our viewers on a global platform.

What have the TASTE AWARDS meant to You? I absolutely love the TASTE AWARDS! I've been inducted into the Hall of Fame and I've also won several awards for several different types of programming from the TASTE AWARDS. I think it's essential that the TASTE AWARDS happens. They are huge contributor to the industry and have made a huge impact in many people's lives on a global scale. I give a huge thank you to all the people who make the TASTE AWARDS possible.

Rocco Leo Gaglioti of FNL Network, photo by Thierry Brouard for Prémium Paris

Yorm Ackuaku

PODCASTER CLOSEUP:
Yorm Ackuaku

Yorm Ackuaku is the founder of esSense 13, a platform working to amplify the work and voices of African food chefs and businesses. In 2018, Yorm launched 'Item 13: An African Food Podcast', a podcast that celebrates the stories of African food entrepreneurs around the world. Item 13 is now part of Heritage Radio Network, America's premier food radio station.

Where are you from originally? Ghana

Where are you based now? I'm currently based in the Washington DC metro area and love this area for its diversity of people, cultures and food.

What is your favorite food or dish? A Ghanaian dish called red-red. It's a flavor-filled tomato-based stewed black eyed peas, served with fried sweet plantains.

What is your favorite restaurant? Such a tough question to answer! I will say, one of my most memorable meals was at Le Virunga in Montreal. The combination of African-inspired dishes and the homey ambiance made it a great experience. One of my favorite brunch spots in the DC area is Busboys and Poets.

Name Your Favorite: Wine, Beer, Cocktail, Juice or Water? These days, it's Bosuo Food's Bissap Rouge. It's an herbal tea inspired by the West African hibiscus drink, bissap.

What is your Favorite City? I've been fortunate to live and work in so many cities around the world. My favorite city living abroad was Johannesburg. In spite of a challenging socio-economic climate, the resilience and beauty of South African people is palpable in this city. Jozi is a vibrant, bustling city with a ton of great food experiences - from local braai's, to sampling South African wine, to visiting Neighborgoods market (a farmers market & brunch destination), you'll be spoiled for choice.

What was the inspiration for the podcast? In my travels around the world, I constantly got asked questions about African food. The questions irked me and I wasn't sure how to answer. At the time, I hadn't traveled much outside of West Africa, so I couldn't speak for the rest of the continent. But I knew of the wide variety of ingredients, flavors, and dishes in the sub-region alone.

I set out to create a platform that celebrated the stories of those creating, curating, and cooking in the African food space. My podcast format was inspired by the podcast, 'How I Built This?'

How did you come up with the name? *Item 13* is Ghanaian slang for food or snacks.

What do you love about it? I love telling the stories of African food entrepreneurs around the world and connecting the dots of their experiences to their dreams of building world-class food products or services.

What is the most challenging part? I interview African food creators from all over the world. The most challenging part is finding a time that works across time zones and making sure it's at a decent time so we can have a great conversation.

How did you go about getting involved or even starting this endeavor from a business or professional standpoint? It didn't take a lot. I've almost always had a full time job along-side the podcast and so had to be creative about having systems that allowed me to record with folks from around the world while

There are a lot of free resources online that I used to get going in the beginning, including Facebook groups of podcasters.

Has it reached your goals for it? Not yet. Being on HRN has opened up a whole new audience for the show. I've been given the opportunity to partner with and or speak on platforms that I wouldn't have had access to before. However, there's still a long way to go in making foods from the African continent more 'mainstream'. I define success for the show as being able to mention 'jollof' or 'red-red' in any company and have no questions asked!

Anything you wish you had known in this industry when you first started? In the food industry, understanding the issues of inequity and how that impacts what ends up on my plate. From a podcasting media perspective, I wish I had known how much post-editing work I would need to do and planned for it better. Maybe it's a good thing I didn't know, otherwise, I may never have started!

Any tips for those aspiring to do better in this media space? Stay true to your mission and everything else will fall into place. It's easy to get discouraged in a crowded media space, but if you have a unique point of view, you will find your tribe.

How much do you use Social Media as part of the business or project? I use social media, particularly Instagram and Twitter, extensively. Instagram is a great visual platform for a food podcast and Twitter helps drive conversations, especially after new episodes air.

What's next for You and this Project? I think it would be great to take the show on the road, to get the opportunity to interact with readers and also share some of the foods from Africa that we talk about on the show.

TRAVEL VLOG CLOSEUP:
The Other Side Vlog

Ian Ryan & Ana are founders and stars of The Other Side Vlog. The two are travel vloggers that have been leaving their footprints around the world while trying to inspire and help people travel.

Where are you from originally? Both Ana & I are from Cleveland, OH

Where are you based now? Tampa, FL

Why? Tampa was a perfect choice because we got to run away from the crazy cold weather in Cleveland during winter months. Because we are travel vloggers, Tampa has one of the best International Airports especially for cheaper tickets. After traveling throughout Florida in our tiny van, we saw how much this state offers. It has natural springs, white sand beaches, hidden gems, and a ton of adventure around every corner. It's a perfect home base for what we do!

What is your Favorite Vacation Spot? If we could go anywhere it would have to be the Philippines. The value you get in this country is unbelievable because we were able to travel it comfortably on $60/day for two people. I mean a bottle of rum is $2 COME ON! It has by far the prettiest water we have seen in our lives, turtles swimming right off the shore on more than 7,000 islands. The friendly locals also make this country unbeatable in our eyes!

What is your Favorite City? Istanbul, Turkey or Belgrade, Serbia

What is your passion? We love traveling and meeting people from all around the world. People energize us every single day. Our passion is helping people travel and we absolutely love making videos and taking pictures

What was the inspiration for The Other Side? We started making Travel YouTube videos 3 years ago because we loved to travel and share our experiences with the entire world. We are inspired by people that have a thirst for travel because that's why we love making videos!

How did you come up with the name? We started dating senior year of high school and then ended up going to separate colleges 10 hours apart from each other (University of South Carolina & Indiana University). Instead of breaking up, we decided to go long distance all 4 years and try to visit on another as much as possible. We decided on "The Other Side" because before we would make that long 10 hour drive to eachother or board that plane, we would text eachother "See you on The Other Side". Bam it made perfect sense because "The Other Side" can mean so many different things especially when you think about travel. "The other side of the world"

What do you love about it? We love connecting with people from different cultures. Learning about food, ways of life, and really putting ourselves into another persons shoes. Travel has taught us literally everything and it definitely made us who we are today

What is the most challenging part? I would say through the past 3 years, it's been all the endless hours working on these videos and building a business from nothing but an idea. We never knew if we would ever make money but dang are we lucky to have an amazing audience. I think the hardest part about being in the social media industry is not knowing if it's going to work out and also the negativity that comes with it. Let's just say if you have videos that do well, people will be commenting and messaging you nasty things even years after you post it. The online world is scary but it has given us freedom I never thought imagined

How did you go about getting involved or even starting this endeavor from a business or professional standpoint? We had an amazing opportunity to study abroad together in Thailand in 2018 and this was a major turning point in our lives. Southeast Asia is where we caught the travel bug and it's also the place where we took a risk and put ourselves out there on YouTube. I would say this trip is when we decided we wanted to become Travel Vloggers after college.

Has it reached your goals for it? We haven't set strict goals but I think just being able to make money doing what you love is success in our book! I would say it felt like forever but came so fast and you never know when you are going to make your dream a reality so don't neglect enjoying your life during the process

Anything you wish you had known in this industry when you first started? I wish we knew early on that perfection is not real. Chasing perfection on our videos and photos always stressed us out too much and made it hard for us to be consistent. As soon as we truly started being ourselves and started posting without the idea of perfection, that's when everything started to fall into place. Learning how to shoot video, edit the videos, take the photos, and start a business is a crazy amount of work so we shouldn't have been so hard on ourselves from the beginning. Learn as much as you can and everything will fall into place down the line!

Any tips for those aspiring to do better in this media space? Perfection will make you burn out. Just learn and keep learning until you start making something you're proud of, then keep going down that road! Also, the only way you can make it in the social media industry is being yourself from the very beginning. If you try to fake your life for a long time, things will catch up to you like burnout and anxiety. Even though it's hard at the beginning, be truly yourself!

How much do you use Social Media as part of the business or project? Every single day but we try to only go on social media for posting our content or quickly commenting/messaging people back. We rarely flip through content because that can be bad for your mental health.

How do you get your ideas for the project? We bounce ideas off each other and have weekly meetings

Who is doing work in this space that you really admire? Lost Leblanc, Brett Conti, Jorden Tually

Do you find that people recognize you on the street? This was the first year where we have had several people stop us on the street because of our big 4 month road trip around the USA in our tiny van. Such a weird/exciting moment whenever this happens

What have the TASTE AWARDS meant to You? Getting a Taste Award was everything for us! It really made us feel special and we are forever thankful for the entire staff and judges at the Taste Awards

LIFESTYLE CELEBRITY CLOSEUP:
Michelle Harris of Alive & Well TV

TASTE AWARD Winner and Celebrity Presenter is the host of Alive & Well with Michelle Harris, a national TV series promoting the wellness lifestyle. Michelle is one of the media's leading lifestyle experts and is a frequent guest on TV shows, radio shows, magazine interviews, red carpets and live events.

Where are you based now? Los Angeles

Why? I am a total California girl! Los Angeles is a beautiful place to live and work. It's also the global center for film and television. It's home.

What is your Favorite Vacation Spot? Carmel, CA. Just a half day drive away from Southern California, but it feels like a different world. It's a relaxing environment and has an amazing coastline.

What is your favorite food or dish? I have to pick just one? I follow a plant based diet and I am a very healthy eater. I love anything with avocado and of course, chocolate!

What is Your Favorite Item of Clothing or Designer? I have many favorite designers. Ronny Kobo, Nookie, Misha Collection, House of CB and you can never get too much Gucci or Chanel. All of which are fur free too!

What is your Camera of Choice? We use Canon C300's a great deal for Alive & Well. Great image quality and a film like feel.

What is your passion? I love creating television content. Being able to help people through communication is a privilege. I am also very passionate about animals and I am part of the animal rescue/advocacy group, Animal Angels.

We started Alive & Well based on our personal lifestyle! I was fortunate enough to combine my work in television with my love of healthy living. It all came together from there!

What do you love about it? I love that we have a television series that has a positive impact on people's health and wellbeing. Anything we can do that improves lives is so rewarding. We also get to have some fun experiences and meet wonderful people at the same time!

How did you go about getting involved or even starting this endeavor from a business or professional standpoint? After college, I was working in television. I formed a company with my husband so we could create content that is important to us. I dug in and took some classes so I knew how to do more work behind the camera, and not just working as talent. Knowing how to produce makes you better in all areas of your job. Now our company develops content we love and would watch ourselves!

Anything you wish you had known in this industry when you first started? When I started, I wish I had known more about the business end of content creation. It's complex but it also helps you find the right opportunities and reach your goals.

Any tips for those aspiring to do better in this media space? Television is growing and even having an explosion of incredible shows. Now, there are even more places to place content than ever before. Just find the home that works for the type of content you are creating!

Who is doing work in this space that you really admire? Rachael Ray has done an incredible job with lifestyle. She has set the bar very high!

Do you find that people recognize you on the street? I do get recognized sometimes. It seems to happen most when I get back from the beach and don't have on any make-up and my hair is a mess. I did meet one of my good friends because he recognized me from the show! We were at the same event and he came up to me. We have a great deal in common so we became friends!

What's next for You and this Project? We are continuing to expand our brand into more television outlets and we have some great new plans!

What have the TASTE AWARDS meant to You? I have been involved with The Taste Awards for a while. I am a member of The Taste Awards Hall of Fame, I have won a Taste Awards and been a host and presenter.

It's the only awards for content creators in lifestyle. The people I have met though The Taste Awards are not only colleagues, but many are now friends. It's a wonderful creative community that I am honored to be a part of.

Michelle Harris

PRODUCER CLOSEUP:
Darley Newman

Recognized in Forbes for her "PBS Travel Empire," Darley Newman is the creator and host of Emmy Award-winning series "Equitrekking" and "Travels with Darley" broadcast on PBS, Amazon Prime, Verizon Digital, Ovation TV and networks in over 85 nations

Where are you from originally? Washington, DC and Myrtle Beach, SC

Where are you based now? New York, NY

What was the inspiration for your television projects? I want to inspire and educate people on how they can find more fulfillment in their lives. That sounds deep from a PBS travel TV series, but I believe that by getting to know people around the world and each other, we become better and more satisfied people... and thus kinder, better humans. It makes for a better world. I've been traveling the world for over a decade filming for my PBS series and various other projects, including Equitrekking and Travels with Darley. It's a passion to share impactful stories that make you think, cry, laugh, learn and grow. I've shared stories of women entrepreneurs in the Middle East, Africa, the USA and Europe, expert historians with knowledge of WWI, Michelin-starred chefs and activists from the civil rights movement... So many great stories that are so important to document and internalize.

What is the most challenging part? We work to create stories that transcend cultural boundaries with a streamlined method of photography and directing using a single camera, which is a challenge. We have to try to weave a tapestry of high-quality sound, visuals and content into "Travels with Darley," directing on camera participants through each documentary-style story, often working with guests who are non-native English speakers in tricky environments. Always, my photographer Greg and I must coordinate scenes on the fly, thinking towards the edit as we conceive each storyline shot with a single camera. Negotiating lighting and environmental sound in real world destinations and scenarios is a challenge, but we work to complete multi-camera look for the series.

How did you go about getting involved or even starting this endeavor from a business or professional standpoint? I wanted to do something that I love on a daily basis. My parents were both entrepreneurs and have also both passed away, so I've seen how short life is. They were both passionate people and I've carried that passion for life and curiosity about the world with me. I want to love what I do and also bring something to other people, which is what I started the "Travels with Darley" series. It took a lot of hard work and creativity to launch my own series, but I believe that all content creators leave a legacy and that can change the world, which is why I love what I do!

Has it reached your goals for it? I have so far, but my goals are always changing. I look forward to continuing to innovate and create, learn and share, continuing to enjoy the diversity of our planet!

Anything you wish you had known in this industry when you first started? You really need to consistently innovate to stay in the media industry. It's been a little like the wild west over the past few years, which I think is exciting, but can also be daunting for an entrepreneur.

Any tips for those aspiring to do better in this media space? Think about your passion and what you want to focus on everyday and translate that into a concept that people will learn from and appreciate. If you can do that, you will find success on some level. Taking it to the next level means continuing to find ways that your work can help others grow. That's an exciting and life-fulfilling proposition.

How much do you use Social Media as part of the business or project? I love using social media to connect with current and new fans and friends. It's such a creative medium through which to share real time and live information and happenings. Over the last few months, I've been able to travel again and film across the USA for our series. I've been focusing on epic trails and history, including the Civil Rights Trail in Alabama, a Revolutionary War Trail around Charleston, South Carolina and more. It's a privilege to be able to hear people's firsthand knowledge and experiences and then share that through my series.

What's next for You and this Project? I'm continuing to film "Travels

with Darley" and this season will complete our 51st half hour! I'm excited to share more great stories of locals across the USA and around the world, as well as continue to think of new ideas for content that will educate and inspire.

What have the TASTE AWARDS meant to You? It's always great to be recognized for your work and achievements. The Taste Awards help shine a light on our wonderful team and our talents in sharing worthwhile stories with the world.

ABOVE: DARLEY NEWMAN

STYLE INFLUENCER CLOSEUP:
Dandy Wellington

Dandy Wellington is a world renowned creator of live and digital experiences. Armed with his love of music and sartorial aesthetics of the past, this Harlem born entertainer, storyteller and style activist specializes in building unique relationships with audiences and brands. Whether he's making appearances at the Sydney Opera House or being featured in The Robb Report and Vogue, Dandy Wellington strives to translate the timeless to a contemporary world.

TASTE: Where are you from originally?

Harlem, New York

TASTE: What is your favorite restaurant?

Gage and Tollner, Maison Pickle, Field Trip

TASTE: What is Your Favorite Item of Clothing or Designer?

Nothing beats a great hat

TASTE: What is your passion?

My biggest passion is bring joy to the world through Jazz, Style and Culture.

TASTE: What was the inspiration for your current projects?

I've always been inspired by the past. Translating an appreciation of history and timeless experiences to people all over the world through music and entertainment.

TASTE: What do you love about it?

I love the opportunity to encourage people to take in the world around them with a sense of the history imbedded in their everyday lives. I love inspiring us all to see the world differently.

TASTE: What is the most challenging part?

The pandemic was the catalyst but also a challenge as it meant I had to create this video experience by myself. I basically learned how to script, shoot, edit and release weekly content as I was doing it. Along the way I discovered an entirely different way to communicate my passions.

TASTE: How did you go about getting involved or even starting this endeavor from a business or professional standpoint?

Research and patience.

I really dove head long into discovering how to integrate this form of digital expression into my business and beyond the technical aspect of the storytelling, I had to ask myself "what kind of stories I wanted to tell". That was my guide.

TASTE: Has it reached your goals for it?

Absolutely not. This kind of work is never finished but that's what makes it so incredible.

TASTE: Any tips for those aspiring to do better in this media space?

Know what you want to say but don't be afraid to discover it along the way.

TASTE: What's next for You and this Project?

In October 2022 I'm hosting vintage style travel experience aboard the Queen Mary II. There will be seminars, socials and events with my 10 piece Jazz band as we travel in style from London to New York.

TASTE: What have the TASTE AWARDS meant to You?

In such a tumultuous year, it's been an honor to be recognized for these achievement. It will serve as welcome motivation to continue to inspire people in new ways.

RIGHT: PHOTO BY JULIA BAHLSEN

CULINARY ICON CLOSEUP:
Diane Kochilas of My Greek Table

In restaurant kitchens, award-winning cookbooks, and her popular, award-winning TV series, My Greek Table on Public Television, Diane has always liked to share the good life and food of Greece and the Mediterranean. She is one of the leading experts on Greek and Mediterranean cooking, a passionate communicator who delves deeply into her subject matter and engages her audience with informative entertainment delivered with liveliness and characteristic immediacy. Diane is the author of more than a dozen cookbooks, an IACP book award winner, the recipient of numerous other book awards, as well as a chef, cooking teacher, and entrepreneur. She runs curated trips to Greece and a recreational cooking school on her native island, the Blue Zone Ikaria, where "people forget to die," as the NYT wrote several years ago.

TASTE: Diane, where are you from originally?

New York City

TASTE: Where are you based now?

Athens, Greece, Ikaria, Greece & New York City

TASTE: Why those places?

I divide my time between three places. On the Blue-Zone Greek island Ikaria, where my family roots are, I run a recreational cooking school and quality-of-life seminars, and spend about 4-5 months a year on the island. New York is my home base for most of the rest of the year, but I also spend time in Athens, running a small culinary walks and tour company and holding events in my kitchen downtown.

TASTE: What is your favorite food or dish?

A perfect summer tomato, warm off the vine, Greek EVOO poured over it, a sprinkling of great tangy feta and some intensely aromatic Greek oregano and sea salt!

TASTE: What is your passion?

Cooking is definitely a passion, as is sharing the wonderful foods, wines, spirits and culture of Greece with the world. But I also love the sea and am a long distance swimmer and novice but passionate sailor. Gardening runs a close second.

TASTE: What was the inspiration for your award-winning television series?

It was always my dream to create a TV series that would share unknown Greece and Greek cuisine with the world. It took a few years to pull it all together, but when My Greek Table was born a few years ago, it was a dream come true.

TASTE: How did you come up with the name?

Trial and error! Long lists and lots of backs and forths with the whole team at Maryland Public Television and Resolution Pictures. The name had to be short, memorable, and to the point. It had to communicate what the show is all about in just a few words. Tables are inviting...Greek tables even more so!

TASTE: What do you love about it?

I love the teamwork. For most of my working life, I was a writer, so worked solo. Even though I worked for a large newspaper in Athens, most of my waking hours were spent alone, researching or writing. But TV production is different. I love the camaraderie and the way we all become a temporary family. I love to feed the crew!

TASTE: What is the most challenging part of the project?

The challenge is always in raising the money -- that's the basic challenge on Public Television.

TASTE: How did you go about getting involved or even starting this endeavor from a business or professional standpoint?

I combed through all the PBS shows I love carefully, vetted their producers, settled on a few and found my partner, Matt. We hit it off immediately. I was intent on doing the series so was glad to find someone who is easy to work with and a great producer!

TASTE: Has My Greek Kitchen reached your goals for it?

Yes, indeed. The show airs all over the USA (96% of the public television market), as well as on Create, Amazon Prime, and internationally in the UK, China, Australia, Canada and Greece. And...we've won a few Taste Awards!

TASTE: What kind of trends are you seeing now in this space?

I think people are more and more interested in plant-based foods and the connection between diet and health.

TASTE: Anything you wish you had known in this industry when you first started?

Hmmm... I wish I had known that on camera we always appear at least 10 pounds heavier!

TASTE: Any tips for those aspiring to do better in this media space?

NEVER GIVE UP! NEVER take No for an an answer!

TASTE: How much do you use Social Media as part of the business or project?

I use it a lot. I am very active on IG/FB and now TikTok. I have great engagement and people turn to my recipes, many from the show, all the time.

TASTE: Any tips for those aspiring to do better in social media?

Publish or perish!

TASTE: How do you get your ideas for the project?

I go with my gut and the things that interest me. I love sharing all the great plant-based recipes of Greece with my audience and they respond positively to that.

TASTE: Who is doing work in this space that you really admire?

Colleagues like Patti Jinlich, Vivian Howard, Lidia Bastianich, Joanne Weir and larger organizations like Milk Street.

TASTE: What's next for You and this Project?

Another season for sure and then...only I and the universe know!

RECIPE.TV CLOSEUP:
Lisa-Renee Ramirez

Lisa-Renee Ramirez is the Executive Vice President of the Lifestyle Networks at Byron Allen's Entertainment Studios - which includes Recipe.TV, MyDestination.TV & Pets.TV. In addition to running the networks, she is the Executive Producer and Director of the networks' multiple award-winning TV series. Lisa-Renee is a winner of 16 Emmy Awards for producing. In May 2020, she was nominated for two Daytime Emmy Awards for "Outstanding Directing for a Single Camera" for two series she created, produced and directed - "Katie Parla's Rome!" and "Vera's Latin America: Panama."

TASTE: Lisa-Renee, where are you from originally?

I'm from Southern California.

TASTE: Where are you based now?

Los Angeles.

TASTE: Why?

It's the center of the entertainment industry.

TASTE: What is your Favorite Vacation Spot?

My home in the Abruzzo region of Italy.

TASTE: What is your favorite restaurant?

Roscioli Salumeria Con Cucina in Rome, Italy.

TASTE: What is Your Favorite Item of Clothing or Designer?

My Max Mara coat!

TASTE: What is your Camera of Choice?

My handy GoPro Hero.

TASTE: Lisa, what is your passion?

Traveling and following my bliss to create entertaining and exciting television.

TASTE: What was the inspiration for your television series on Recipe.TV?

I am a Francophile. I lived in the Burgundy region of France when I was younger, and have always dreamed of sharing my love of the French markets, culinary classics and culture of that wonderful country with viewers at home. Many people dream of going to Paris or Rome. I wanted to create a series that transports viewers to these beautiful, far away places that they may never get a chance to visit themselves.

TASTE: How did you come up with the names?

The first series that I created for our Recipe.TV channel was "A Parisian Food Affair with Julie Neis." Our host Julie is a culinary influencer, and her blog was titled "Paris Food Affair." Since I have my own love affair with Paris, we came up with the title "A Parisian Food Affair with Julie Neis." It sounds romantic and captivating, just like the show.

TASTE: What do you love about it?

I love the challenge of telling compelling and entertaining stories. Some of my favorite parts of my job include discovering exciting new talent, creating the looks and aesthetics of our shows, showcasing delectable dishes and inspiring people at home to make them themselves, all while transporting viewers to new and exciting locations. It's all a part of this sometimes difficult but ultimately satisfying creative process.

TASTE: What is the most challenging part?

All of the series I've created are shot on location in countries around the world - from Paris to Rome - to Panama and Dublin - and there are challenges that come with managing foreign crews, navigating bustling cities, and creating shows in places where I don't speak the language fluently.

TASTE: How did you go about getting involved or even starting this endeavor from a business or professional standpoint?

I had been creating content for Byron Allen's Entertainment Studios television networks - including Pets.TV and MyDestination.

TV - and in 2018, I added Recipe.TV to my plate as well, and made it my goal to bring an international flavor to the network! In addition to finding the content compelling myself, I wanted to ensure that Recipe.TV stands apart from other networks in our genre.

TASTE: Has it reached your goals for it?

I'm happy to say that our first series out of the gate for Recipe.TV - "A Parisian Food Affair with Julie Neis" - won the coveted Taste Award for "Best New Series" in 2019. This was incredibly validating - and encouraging. It gave us confidence to keep moving in the right direction.

In the next few years we went on to receive several TASTE AWARD nominations and multiple TASTE AWARDS including getting inducted in to the TASTE AWARDS Hall of Fame in 2020. In addition, we've received four Emmy nominations over three consecutive years. I'm thankful to God for the abundant blessings that have come from following my heart.

TASTE: What kind of trends are you seeing now in this space?

The streaming networks have gotten into the food and recipe game.

TASTE: Anything you wish you had known in this industry when you first started?

I've learned to speak up for myself and ask for what I need. You'd be surprised at the support that appears when you begin to take bold action that aligns with your values.

TASTE: Any tips for those aspiring to do better in this media space?

Only be in competition with yourself and nobody else. Don't settle. Always aim to improve, and never rest on your laurels. Remember, every shot counts.

TASTE: Any tips for those aspiring to do better in social media?

People respond to authenticity. Keep it simple and sincere.

TASTE: Who is doing work in this space that you really admire?

Nadiya Hussain - a chef who won the Great British Bake Off. I love her shows on Netflix.

TASTE: What's next for You and this Project?

We have a wonderful, fresh new show with one of our Emmy-nominated chefs that will be premiering in the fall, and we've got a very exciting new host and series in a fabulous new international destination that begins filming next month. Stay tuned to Recipe.TV as we continue to grow and expand the network.

TASTE: What have the TASTE AWARDS meant to You?

The TASTE AWARDS mean the world to me! They put Recipe.TV on the map, and for that we're extremely grateful. We can't to wait to see what's next for The TASTE AWARDS.

PEOPLE TO KNOW:
BEHIND THE SCENES AT HOLLYWOOD RED CARPET EVENTS

LONDON MOORE
FOUNDER, CRC
CELEBRITY RED CARPETS

You can't have a red carpet event without lights, a step and repeat area including background graphics and a red carpet, maybe some stanchions, and someone to set it all up professionally and on time. CRC is well known in Hollywood for getting the job done on time and professionally.

London Moore is an entrepreneur that has been working in Los Angeles for more than 20 years from handling event production, running a management company for models, dancers and choreographers to the continued hustle to handle some of the top events and networking parties this town has ever seen.

If you've gone to any event at the W in Hollywood or the Sofitel in Beverly Hills chances are you've seen London Moore. If you've been to any networking event under the label SocialMixLA chances are you've seen London Moore. And if you've stepped on any "step and repeat" that is professionally done chances are you've seen London Moore.

To most a "step and repeat" is just a slab of red carpet and a large banner with poles holding it up but to London it was a chance to create a name for himself. So 10 years ago he completely threw away that basic mold and started building and creating custom spec carpets and backdrops under the label Celebrity Red Carpets. "It's the first thing people see and it's the first thing people try to get in front of... I wanted to make sure it was a reflection of myself and my company and keep the standards higher than the competition" London says.

Celebrity Red Carpets, was an easy transition from the event planning side as the demand for professional, well done and creative step and repeats started becoming the norm in Los Angeles. London had to expand quickly with clientele looking for more than the average carpet and banner setup and well known companies such as AMC, Netflix, Disney, BET Network, Fox and of course Marvel wanted to work with only London. London found a way to take something that was overlooked and worked hard to be the best at it.

TASTEABLE
SECTION: ART & DESIGN

TASTE PHOTO AWARDS

THE FINALISTS

Fantastic photography can cover a lot of territory. The TASTE PHOTOS AWARDS honors those focusing on the topics of Food, Wine & Spirits Fashion & Design, Travel, and Health & Exercise. This year the TASTE PHOTO AWARDS spotlight the following great compositions by the most recent awards finalists from around the world.

THIS PAGE
Henriette and Toby Wulff – Crème brûlée
Alyssa Nelson – Cocktail

Abdullah Al Kandari, "The Obscure Dandelions"

Alyssa Nelson, "Cocktail"

April McClure, "Southern California Piers"

Bozena Garbinska, "Grapes"

Claudio D´Attis, "Twins, 6 Image Series"

Devin DePamphilis, "Jumping in Ice Cream"

Dilip Khatri, "Cactus Lane"

Henriette and Toby Wulff, "Crème brûlée"

James Cavanah, -Bradley Lamb"

Matt Armendariz, "Abalone Carpaccio, Jordan Winery"

Michelle Ullmann, "Girl and Her Wolf"

Muneer Majeed, "Mushroom Soup with Toasted Bread"

Nicholas Powell "A Storm in Utah"

Peter Irgens, Charlotte Andersen, "Age is just a number"

Peter Irgens, Charlotte Andersen, "Nutcracker twenty20 Part A & Part B"

Wendy Bednarz, "Surma, ARTifice Traces Suri in Present"

Xu Han, "Food"

Xu Han, "I Think They belong on Vogue"

James Cavanah, "Bradley Lamb"

Bozena Garbinska, "Grapes"

THIS PAGE: Dilip Khatri, "Cactus Lane"

OPPOSITE PAGE: Peter Irgens, Charlotte Andersen, "Nutcracker twenty20 Part B"

ABOVE: Wendy Bednarz, "Surma, ARTifice Traces Suri in Present" BELOW: Peter Irgens, Charlotte Andersen, "Age is just a number" OPPOSITE PAGE: Nicholas Powell "A Storm in Utah"

ABOVE: April McClure, "Southern California Piers", BELOW: Claudio D´Attis, "Twins, 6 Image Series"
OPPOSITE PAGE: Michelle Ullmann, "Girl and Her Wolf"

ABOVE:
Abdullah Al Kandari, "The Obscure Dandelions"

RIGHT:
Xu Han, "Food"

OPPOSITE PAGE TOP:
Muneer Majeed, "Mushroom Soup with Toasted Bread"

OPPOSITE PAGE BOTTOM:
Peter Irgens, Charlotte Andersen, "Nutcracker twenty20 Part A "

ABOVE:
Xu Han – "I think they belong on vogue"

OPPOSITE PAGE TOP:
Matt Armendariz, "Abalone Carpaccio, Jordan Winery"

OPPOSITE PAGE BOTTOM:
Devin DePamphilis, "Jumping in Ice Cream"

MUSICIANS IN THE SPOTLIGHT
THE SEARCH FOR INSPIRATION

Harrison Tinsley

"What inspires me? Courage. I'm inspired by the stories we hear of people who had all that odds against them, who had everybody doubting them, who had plenty of chances to quit, but chose to keep going not knowing what would happen. I believe that being brave is the most important virtue. Music has been there for me when I have been happy and sad, whether my day was good or bad. It gives me chills when I listen and relate to a song, sometimes it makes me feel invincible. I hope some of my songs can inspire others to be brave, to help people feel less alone, to help them fall in love. I will always have the courage to write songs that mean something and chase my dreams."

Harrison Tinsley is a singer-songwriter and rocker from California. His songs strike through your heart with a profound sense of vulnerability and meaning. When you see him live you can't help but want to sing along and you can tell he means it. He's rocked regularly from up north in Lake Tahoe to down south in San Diego. His song "Be Brave" was awarded in the International Songwriters Day competition for best inspirational song and his song "Emily" won the California Music Video Award for best love song. He was also seen on American Idol. New music is coming from him soon. Currently he is in the bay area where he grew up.

THIS PAGE: HARRISON TINSLEY
OPPOSITE PAGE: MAVENNE

Mavenne

"I am inspired by other artists and their music production which grows me as an artist. I'm also inspired by other art forms such as modern architecture and interior design which creates a futuristic sci-fi feel and really put me in the mood to write and produce new songs; I really love to produce! Nature also gives me a lot of inspiration as you can see in my music video for Faraway Far which has places like Malibu that have always filled me with inspiration. Since I've traveled quite a bit, I'm frequently inspired by new places and scenery so I wanted to tie that into my first music video."

Alternative-pop singer-songwriter & producer Mavenne [maven] started out as a classical singer. Her vocals as a young child were favorably compared to Charlotte Church. Tragically, a childhood illness resulted in the loss of her voice at the age of 9 and it was during that time that she turned to songwriting at her keyboard, even while she underwent nine months of vocal therapy with the same speech therapist who helped restore the voice of Sound of Music star Julie Andrews. Mavenne's voice has since flourished and she also developed a talent for producing after training with former head of A & R for Capitol Records, Loren Israel. She has won such prestigious competitions as the California Music Video Awards, The John Lennon Songwriting Contest (for Pop), The International Acoustic Music Awards (as a "Top Ten Alternative Artist" for vocal performance) & more recently has had her music featured on The CW TV show Batwoman. Mavenne's music has been influenced by such power-house singers as Lana Del Rey, Marina, and Sia. Readers may get an exclusive song download at Mavenne.com

Jon Mullane

"I'm inspired by my observations of the human condition, the creativity of the soul and our coexistence with nature: crafting a great melody and lyric out of seemingly nowhere; a beautiful painting arising from a blank canvas; the building of a house from wood and nails; a random act of kindness between strangers; the bond between animal and human; the waves crashing into the seashore – these things and many others are what inspire me."

Jon Mullane is an award winning, Billboard charting singer, songwriter & performer originally hailing from Halifax, NS Canada. He has gained International acclaim and attention through his music, as his songs have been heard on commercial radio stations, featured in numerous television shows, films and commercials and played at International sporting events. Heralded for his strong melodic sense, Jon Mullane defines what an artist is...embracing an unbridled passion for and dedication to his music combined with an authenticity that connects him with his fans.

THE CALIFORNIA MUSIC VIDEO AWARDS

The music & film industry have an undeniable connection to California. Sometimes it's the passion, sometimes it's the vision, sometimes it's the style, and sometimes it's the sound. That is the reason for the CALIFORNIA MUSIC VIDEO AWARDS.

The CALIFORNIA MUSIC VIDEO AWARDS celebrate some of the year's most exciting and creative music videos, music, musicians, artists, films and directors from around the world. They honor that great work and musical connection. The awards are for music videos, music films and documentaries. www.MusicalVideoAwards.com

JON MULLANE

The Christopher Brothers

"We are super inspired everyday by our amazing fans!. Performing is our favorite thing to do, and nothing is more exhilarating than when a person is vibing with your music, and everything else in the world just disappears. Without music and performing I believe we would feel very lost and we are thankful that we are able to continue sharing our music with everyone."

The Christopher Brothers is an alternative pop/rock band from Los Angeles, CA. The band has an international following with over 4 million views on YouTube, 440,000 Facebook "Likes", and 70,000 Twitter Followers.Their album, "Dog Daze" featuring the single "Let Me Out", debuted at No.7 on Billboards Hot Single Sales Chart and ultimately made it to No. 68 on the Top 40 Radio Media Base Chart. In addition The Christopher Brothers' music, "And Now I'm In Love Again" from their EP "Smile", has played at retail venues throughout the US. The band made it to the top 20 of the group category on X Factor with great praises from Simon Cowell on their original song "Smile." Their music video "The Girl Next Door" also won the "California Music Video Best Band Award". Since the brothers formed their band, they have toured extensively throughout the United States performing at venues including the world famous Whisky a Go Go, The Roxy, LEGOLAND California, Six Flags, and the Time Warner Center in NYC. The brothers have opened for The Plain White T's and Drake Bell on the High School Nation Tour doing hundreds of shows with Hollister and Ernie Ball as Sponsors. The Christopher Brothers also regularly perform at Downtown Disney.

Xavier Toscano

"What inspires me? Life! With it's wonders, trials, and surprises! There's no end to how much you can draw from your daily experiences."

Xavier's music is influenced by Top 40 Billboard. It can best be described as enthusiastic, energetic, dance-urban pop. He also blends his love of EDM, rap, rock, reggae, and R&B with his dancing ability to create a dynamic stage show. Wherever Xavier performs, he is always praised for having a "ton of energy." Combine that with his strong stage presence, and you have well rounded entertainer who puts on electric and engaging show.

Monumental sculpture "Rocket" by Hubert Phipps at the Boca Raton Innovation Campus (BRiC), the historic tech landmark where the first IBM Personal Computer was invented. The Phipps sculpture is valued at $1.5 million, stands 30-feet tall, weighs 9.8 tons, and took more than 2,200 square feet of stainless steel to construct.

Christ Natrop "In the Fold"
Exhibition at the
Nancy Toomey Fine Art

THE ART OF COLLECTING ART

In the past the wealthy were able to surround themselves completely with objects of beauty: paintings, furniture, homes, chariots, horses, and even people. Thus is the benefit of wealth. But the appreciation of beauty is not limited to any particular economic class or social order, and there are many forms of art which appeal to a range of tastes and interests.

It is a natural human desire that when you find something that meets your tastes you have but one immediate aspiration: to possess it. That is the origin of collecting.

But the foundation of this aspiration goes much further than simple possession, because by collecting you are also making a personal commitment to protect and preserve that particularly piece of art, support the artist, and hopefully, share the work's inherent spirit with others. Incidentally, you may actually see an appreciation in your collection's value over time.

If you find yourself in the collecting mood, the following interviews with experts will give you some good advice and recommendations.

COLLECTING ART BOOKS

Recommended Fine Art Photography Books for your Library

As photography has gained acceptance as a collectible fine art form, so have photography books. A less expensive alternative than the purchase of an actual photographic print, some $75-$150 fine art photography books nevertheless can increase in value to $500-$10,000 over a period of as little as five years. In addition, collecting the books of photographer can often be the beginning of collecting their work. But as with all art, it is better to collect what inspires you personally, rather than chase a particular investment. The following are some titles that we recommend. (Note, because prices change frequently, we have left off the current market values for these publications.)

Top Left: "Please Return Polaroid" by Miles Aldridge, published by Edition Z Paris

Top Right: "Zanele Muholi," Editor Allen Sarah, and Yasufumi Nakori, published by Tate Publishing/Abrams

Right: "Resident Dog: Incredible Homes and the Dogs That Live There" by Nicole England. Published by Thames & Hudson

Bottom Right: "American Protest: Photographs 2020 - 2021" by Mel D. Cole, Introduction by Jamie Lee Curtis, published by Damiani

Bottom: "The Goldfinger Files: The Making of the Iconic Alpine Sequence in the James Bond Movie Goldfinger" by Steffen Appel, published by Steidl

Bottom Left: "Selected Works" by Vincent Peters, published by teNeues

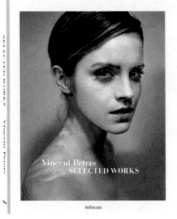

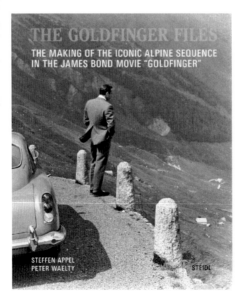

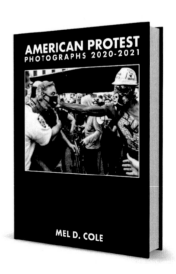

Opposite Page: Image from the book "Please Return Polaroid" by Miles Aldridge, published by Edition Z Paris

Image from the book "Please Return Polaroid" by Miles Aldridge, published by Edition Z Paris

Image from the book "Please Return Polaroid" by Miles Aldridge, published by Edition Z Paris

Image from the book "Resident Dog: Incredible Homes and the Dogs That Live There," by Nicole England. Published by Thames & Hudson

Image from the book "Resident Dog: Incredible Homes and the Dogs That Live There," by Nicole England. Published by Thames & Hudson

Images from the book "The Goldfinger Files: The Making of the Iconic Alpine Sequence in the James Bond Movie Goldfinger," by Steffen Appel, Published by Steidl

Image from the book "American Protest: Photographs 2020 - 2021," by Mel D. Cole, Introduction by Jamie Lee Curtis, published by Damiani

Image from the book "American Protest: Photographs 2020 - 2021," by Mel D. Cole, introduction by Jamie Lee Curtis, published by Damiani

Image from the books "Selected Works" and "The Light Between Us" by Vincent Peters, published by teNeues

APPLE STORE @ APPLE PARK
A DESIGN MECCA FOR TECH LOVERS

If you have an Apple device or computer then you know that at some point you are going to visit an Apple store. The stores are not just attractive places to shop, they are also a very useful resource. Prior to Apple's opening of its own chain of retail and support outlets, the only way to really get service for a Mac was to find a local dealer or firm that specialized in this niche brand. Fortunately, Apple is no longer a niche brand, and you can get support anywhere you need as long as there's an Apple store around.

There are many great designs for Apple stores around the world, including one in Los Angeles inside of a historic movie theater. Nonetheless, any visit near the Apple headquarters in Apple Park means you absolutely must stop by the Apple Visitor Center store. The Apple Park Visitor Center opened in November 2017, and as a destination has seen thousands of shoppers and Apple fans. The entire Apple Park campus is over 175-acres. In many ways the Visitor Center looks just like a regular Apple store, except it is more grand in scale. It has more windows, more open spaces, more high ceilings, a working cafeteria, and a general feeling of serenity and destination.

The Visitor Center was designed by Foster + Partners, who also created buildings and elements of the overall Apple campus. In that vein, the Visitor Center contains many of the same architectural details as the actual Apple campus offices, including the designs for staircases, stonewalls and Terrazzo floors. The Center is also fully encased by meters-high floor to ceiling glass walls, allowing in not only an outstanding amount of natural light, but also a feeling that the Center is an extension of the outdoor environment. This is key, because most Apple stores are not surrounded by tree-lined parks, but

this one is. As such, the visitor feels as if they are in a very special place, and they know that this place is located at the center of the Apple Universe.

The Visitor Center uses a cantilevered carbon roof as well as lovely natural wood. The top floor is dedicated to a terrace area which overlooks the wooded campus. It provides beautiful views, as well as lovely sunsets. The terrace roof is shaded by carbon fiber fins that offer varying and pleasant amounts of shade, while not obstructing the view. The upstairs terrace includes tables for lunch or outdoor meetings. The stairwell and staircases are made of quartz stone.

Not many Apple stores have their own cafés, but this one does. It offers coffee and snacks, including a selection of high-end luxury artisan chocolate. The café's countertop is made of marble, and the entire café looks directly outward to a grove of olive trees.

The Visitor Center also has a 3-D model of the entire campus,

for those who cannot enter the actual Apple office buildings but would like to appreciate the design space that Apple has created for its employees. Guided tours led by docents and employees are available for fans who want to know more.

Apple Park Visitor Center
10600 North Tantau Avenue
Cupertino, CA 95014

REPORT: GEAR

ALUMINUM M1 WIRELESS MOUSE
Satechi

If you're tired of not having the Right Click button on your mouse, as well as it just looking like a lump of plastic all day, then this high-tech mouse from Satechi has features that will make your desktop a lot more stylish and functional. The M1 is made in smooth and modern aluminum, with a black contrasting area for the selection wheel/button. It is easily connected via Bluetooth with a range of up to 32 feet, and can be recharged using the Type-C port. The M1 is also very quick and precise, with optical sensors and 1200 DPI resolution. One extra perk, it is good for right or left handed users.

www.Satechi.net

LIMITED EDITION TESLACOIL PEN
Michael's Pens

You don't have to be a geek to love the details and craftsmanship of this lovely pen. Completely made and manufactured in the United States, using advanced machining methods, it is hard not to admire. Created in honor of Nikola Tesla, a scientist who inspired Science-fiction movies, inventors, electric cars, and contributed to the alternating current aspects of our electrical system. This pen looks good in your hand, as well as proudly on display.

www.MichaelsPens.com

REPORT: EYEWEAR

BOOKER

COLLINS

RORY

ROKA SUNGLASSES
Roka Sports

We're always big fans of ROKA Sunglasses, and our selections this edition include the very cool new models called BOOKER, COLLINS, AND RORY. Even if these weren't great sunglasses, they would still have great names.

They of course have some of the regular features you would expect with ROKA, such as:

- High Strength-to-Weight Ratio, Strong Environmental Stress and Corrosion Resistance
- Premium C3™ Nylon Lenses aith Anti-Scratch, Anti-Fog and Anti-Reflectance Coatings
- Super-Hydrophobic and Oleophobic Coatings for Anti-Spotting, Fingerprint Resistance, and Easy Cleaning

www.Roka.com

Owls have amazing eyesight and optical range. Above is Albus the Barn Owl, a member of the pigeon abatement team at Full Circle Falconry in the San Francisco Bay Area

STYLE: EDITORS CHOICE

This Page & Opposite: From the TATRAS Fall/Winter collection (shot at the iconic James Goldstein Residence, an architectural staple in Los Angeles)

This Page & Opposite: From the TATRAS Fall/Winter collection (shot at the iconic James Goldstein Residence, an architectural staple in Los Angeles)

This Page & Opposite: From the TATRAS Fall/Winter collection (shot at the iconic James Goldstein Residence, an architectural staple in Los Angeles)

THIS PAGE & OPPOSITE: RODARTE X TOM PETTY CAPSULE COLLECTION COLLABORATION IN CELEBRATION OF TOM PETTY'S "WILDFLOWERS." PHOTO CREDIT: DARIA KOBAYASHI RITCH

WEEKENDER BAG: Any road trip or journey can be stylish with the 'Steve McQueen by INHERENT' weekender bag. Performance is ensured with YKK zippers, custom zipper pulls, and style provided by the black leather exterior with racing red stitching and racing red leather interior.

DRIVING GLOVES: Control the steering wheel with these Black Peccary Leather Driving Gloves that carry INHERENT's Racing Red colored Piping. Handmade in Napoli, Italy, by specialist driving-glove craftsmen.

TOP COAT: Steve McQueen is known to wear a sand car coat in the movies *The Thomas Crown Affair* and *Bullitt*. This Car Coat is designed to fit, taking styling cues from the movies with a fresh spin. Fabric: 100% Tan Cotton

All from **INHERENT**, the online custom menswear shop, www.ThisIsInherent.com

Actress, Producer and award-winning television host Andrea Feczko with Vessel Signature 2.0 Boston Duffel Bag

FARHAD RE
COUTURE COLLECTION PRINTEMPS ÉTÉ SPRING SUMMER
© Greg Alexander - Méphistophélès Productions

NAJIB ALIOUA
COLLECTION COUTURE AUTOMNE HIVER
FALL WINTER

PERFUMER PROFILE

Christi Meshell
House of Matriarch

TASTEABLE: Christi, where are you based?

I'm in Seattle, Washington

TASTEABLE: Were you always a fragrance fan, or was it something that you discovered?

Scent was always a focus of my attention, even as a child. It was not until I was in my 30's that I realized I had a talent for fragrance arrangements.

TASTEABLE: Are there any key ingredients that you like to use regularly?

Yes, I love using a wide spectrum of cedars. I use some form of cedar in just about every composition - there are so many different aromas in the species, not just the "sauna" aroma. My favorite top note is plai, it comes from central Thailand and is rumored to be the "secret ingredient" in Oil of Olay. Also rose - impossible to replace and also a part of almost every creation.

TASTEABLE: What do you look for when you are creating new artisan scents?

Something novel enough to be intriguing but familiar enough to be acceptable to the palate - it's a delicate balance.

TASTEABLE: If you made a new uni-sex fragrance, how would it smell?

Like a late-night tea party with your favorite friends!

TASTEABLE: What are you thinking about doing over the next few years?

Greatly looking forward to the launch of my high spirits line - I've been fine tuning my blends for years and looking forward to the upcoming launch of a few debut vintages.

FRAGRANCE GURU

Sebastian Jara
The Perfume Guy

TASTEABLE: Where are you based?

San Francisco, CA

TASTEABLE: Were you always a fragrance fan, or was it something that you discovered?

Yes, always since I was a kid but it got more and more exciting as I got older. Now I'm obsessed with scent.

TASTEABLE: They call you a guru of scent. How does one become a fragrance guru?

I think once people realize that you are recommending them great fragrances they start coming back to you for more suggestions and others follow them and follow me and soon you have a following and people trust you for your recommendations. Something like that.

TASTEABLE: You have a rather large fan base of followers. What is the most popular topic you cover?

I speak a lot about Patchouli and Vanilla Fragrances on the channel among many other topics.

TASTEABLE: What do you look for when seeking out and trying new artisan scents?

Wearability. If I can't wear it I'm not going to speak about it let alone buy it. So it must be wearable. It can be challenging to an extent but still must be wearable.

TASTEABLE: Are there any exciting trends you are seeing right now?

I'm seeing florals, green, vanilla, fruits as trends but I also see minimalistic and happy uplifting scents as being trendy as well.

PERFUMER PROFILE

Olivia Larson
La Fleur by Livvy

TASTEABLE: Christi, where are you based?

I'm in Seattle, Washington

TASTEABLE: Were you always a fragrance fan, or was it something that you discovered?

Scent was always a focus of my attention, even as a child. It was not until I was in my 30's that I realized I had a talent for fragrance arrangements.

TASTEABLE: Are there any key ingredients that you like to use regularly?

Yes, I love using a wide spectrum of cedars. I use some form of cedar in just about every composition - there are so many different aromas in the species, not just the "sauna" aroma.

My favorite top note is plai, it comes from central Thailand and is rumored to be the "secret ingredient" in Oil of Olay.

Also rose - impossible to replace and also a part of almost every creation.

TASTEABLE: What do you look for when you are creating new artisan scents?

Something novel enough to be intriguing but familiar enough to be acceptable to the palate - it's a delicate balance.

TASTEABLE: If you made a new uni-sex fragrance, how would it smell?

Like a late-night tea party with your favorite friends!

TASTEABLE: What are you thinking about doing over the next few years?

Greatly looking forward to the launch of my high spirits line - I've been fine tuning my blends for years and looking forward to the upcoming launch of a few debut vintages.

SCENTS: EDITORS CHOICE

LEFT: La Fleur by Livvy A Walk in Giverny Natural EDP (BRONZE MEDAL)

IN ORDER, LEFT TO RIGHT:
PK Perfumes Charis (BRONZE MEDAL), Pomare's Stolen Perfume Piano Tuner 2020 (BRONZE MEDAL), La Fleur by Livvy NUR (BRONZE MEDAL), Elia Parfum Amalfi (BRONZE MEDAL), Jade Daisy Perfumes Violeta (SILVER MEDAL), Jade Daisy Perfumes Lola (BRONZE MEDAL), Jade Daisy Perfumes Siva (SILVER MEDAL), La Grange du Parfumeur Murmuration (GOLD MEDAL), La Fleur by Livvy A Walk in Giverny Natural EDP (BRONZE MEDAL), S ENT NUDES Love in the Time of Corona // Eau de Parfum (BRONZE MEDAL), ENVOYAGE Zhivago (SILVER MEDAL)

OTHER SELECTIONS (Not Pictured):
House of Matriarch Vanilla Caviar (GOLD MEDAL), BY MARILIIS Fier Rose (SILVER MEDAL), Pomare's Stolen Perfume For You, My Love (BRONZE MEDAL), Elia Parfum No. 1 (BRONZE MEDAL), PK Perfumes Cheery Blossom (BRONZE MEDAL), Pomare's Stolen Perfume Heiva In Solitude (BRONZE MEDAL), House of Matriarch Black Sheep (BRONZE MEDAL)

REVIEWER'S COMMENTS: Scents are our most sensitive olfactory, it has a direct pathway to our brain. It elicits our most primitive emotions and deepest memories.

REVIEWER'S COMMENTS: "Love in Time of Corona". Havana is filled with streets of old world architecture preserved in time. After sunset one nite, I heard a wooing lover, " Maricela, I'm here, come down.""

REVIEWER'S COMMENTS: I felt like I loved Elia Parfum No. 1 and Amalfi equally. They were the most polished and complete fragrances and smelled perfect to me out of all of the samples. Followed by the selections of House Of Matriarch.

REVIEWER'S COMMENTS: Nur by Livvy is one of her best fragrances; It tells her story and her connection to India. I applaud several of the perfumers who are creating scents with a cause, especially Elia giving proceeds to fight sex trafficking. I am not the biggest citrus fan but Elia Almalfi takes me to Positano as its sun-soaked character evokes limoncello. I am crazy for all of Pomare's fragrance and love that she is a sommelier, and I want For You My Love as a cocktail! House of Matriarch's Black Sheep is innovative and strange at the same time. How on earth did she think to extract a scent from sheep wool?! While I absolutely love By Mariliis Fler Rose, my husband couldn't stop smelling it on me! What an exciting and unusual rose scent, with smoky notes, jammy red fruit and a buttery creamy dry down.

REVIEWER'S COMMENTS: Murmuration by La Grange du Parfumeur: Deep, sophisticated, sweet, but not cloying, mood-elevating and invigorating! Great job! Elia No 1 is really number One, period. Lovely Charis and Cheery Blossom from PK Perfumes, which is no surprise given the time-proven mastery of the perfumer. A Walk in Giverny from La Fleur by Livvy-excellent!

MICKELA MALLOZZI, "BARE FEET WITH MICKELA MALLOZZI" (NATIONAL TELEVISION SERIES), HOST & EXECUTIVE PRODUCER

INSPIRATIONS
A LOOKBOOK OF RISING TASTEMAKERS

Striving to be a truly relevant Tastemaker — aka, a person who influences others opinions, ideas, or lifestyle — takes a lot of work. This work doesn't just restrict itself to doing projects, making plans, implementing strategies, sacrificing personal and professional investments of time and money, and essentially everything else needed to get things done.

Being a truly relevant Tastemaker also comes down to having a great personality, an ability to emphasize with others, and evolving communication skills. Sometimes it also requires presenting an interesting image to the public. It goes without saying that anyone in the business will tell you that a good headshot might take you very far... or at the very least it could open a few doors. That's why we like to take this opportunity to present a Lookbook of some of our favorite rising Tastemakers. They range from television and film to music and social media.

Photographs courtesy of each Tastemaker

LIZ MAREK OF @SUGARGEEKSHOW, INFLUENCER AND CAKE DECORATOR

NATHAN WITTE, FILM AND TELEVISION ACTOR. AKA Steel Afro the Spoken Lyricist

THE FOOD NANNY

Lizi Heaps
@TheFoodNanny,
Host, Producer,
Instagram Influencer

TASTEABLE
SECTION: FOOD & DRINK

SITKA SALMON SHARES

"OCEAN TO TABLE" IS A RAPIDLY GROWING OPTION FOR FRESH SEAFOOD DELIVERED DIRECTLY TO CONSUMERS

Over the last few years there have been a number of local seafood groups that have come together to begin shipping fresh or frozen seafood directly to the end-user. This is not a coincidence, considering how many people are now working from home and cooking at home. It also reflects the fact that the restaurant buyers and wholesale buyers that used to purchase these harvests are now doing so in lesser amounts. The seafood groups have therefore pivoted to a new business model which really makes a lot of sense, especially considering evolving online shopping behaviors and product delivery options.

One of our first impressions about the Sitka Salmon Shares package we tested was that each selection of fish was quite thick. These were not thin fillets, these were 1 to 2 inch sized pieces. This was not only impressive and felt like a better value, but also presented new opportunities as far as potential recipes. One recipe we used for example was to lightly marinate a halibut in a sesame ginger dressing purchased from Whole Foods. After this piece was marinated for two hours, it was baked in the oven, and produce a fantastically delicious, restaurant-quality dish.

The Sitka Shares wild caught salmon was exactly the same. Thick, and even when frozen was still appealingly reddish in color. This fish did not look like it had been sitting more than a few moments after having been caught before it was frozen and sealed up for delivery.

This highlights one of the great benefits of getting your fish directly from those who catch them. The time between having been caught and being sent to you is greatly reduced, and what arrives is of a higher quality, as well as reflects the pride in those people doing the work. In other words, you feel confident that they are not going send you something that is sub par just to make a buck. They want you to believe in what they do, so that you keep coming back.

We chatted with the folks at Sitka Salmon Shares to get more insight into their operations.

TASTEABLE: When was Sitka Salmon Shares founded? Who came up with the idea?

Sitka Salmon Shares was founded in 2011 where a Midwestern college professor, Nic Mink, and his students traveled to Stika, Alaska. They returned to the Midwest with boxes of line-caught, wild Alaska salmon, harvested by their fisher friends in Sitka. People raved about the salmon's taste and were impressed by its traceability. They quickly made the connection between their consumption and the impact this small act could have on conservation efforts and the health of Alaska's responsibly managed fisheries.

During their trip, Nic and his students met Marsh. Marsh was the self-styled foodie and passionate gourmand of Sitka's hook-and-line salmon fleet. A local legend on the Sitka dinner party circuit, Marsh's favorite pastime included sourcing ingredients from the wilds of Southeast Alaska and elevating them with techniques learned from stints in professional kitchens.

As you might suspect, Marsh's quest for perfect food spilled into his work as a commercial fisherman. He obsessively handled his fish every step of the way to guarantee that eaters on the other end of his line enjoyed the perfection he sought in his own kitchen—including his family down in the proud town of Green Bay, Wisconsin.

Sitka Salmon Shares is now a completely integrated boat-to-doorstep seafood company. We have a lovable group of fishermen-owners who deliver our fish. We have a small processing plant in Sitka, Alaska, where we custom-process our catch with a laser focus on quality and traceability. And we have two Good-Fish Hubs in the Midwest, which allow us to deliver our fishermen's catch directly to your doorstep (or to your local farmers market or restaurant).

TASTEABLE: Direct to consumer seafood has really taken off since 2020, several firms are now doing it. Why do you think that is?

Sitka Salmon Shares experienced unexpected growth during 2020 due to the global pandemic. In the early months of lockdown there were shortages of many proteins, including seafood. This demand drove many to look for delivery options like Sitka Salmon Shares. Many of our new subscribers enjoyed the quality and convenience of our shares to continue enrolling.

2020's increased interest also coincided with the popularity of becoming a more conscious consumer. Many shoppers are more aware of the impacts of the goods and products they enjoy. With the company's CSF model and transparency, subscribers are joining a community of artisan fishers, healthy eaters, foodies, and Alaskan adventurers in our collective efforts to rebuild America's seafood system from the ground up. All of us together are actively supporting responsibly sourced seafood and independent, family fishermen who fish in much the same way their grandparents did.

TASTEABLE: How does Sitka Salmon Shares work?

Members purchase "shares" of the catch, similar to paying for a share of the harvest from a local farm through your favorite CSA. Members receive a monthly home seafood

delivery that ranges from 4.5 to 5 pounds. Shares are delivered from April through December, the fishing season, to provide the highest quality wild seafood.

Our product is caught using responsible fishing practices like hook and line by small-boat fishermen.

TASTEABLE: Are the shares like equity, or like when you pre-order shares of a wine before it's made?

A "share" is no different than a subscription. Buyers have the choice of purchasing their full share in one payment or monthly installments. During the fall, Sitka Salmon Shares runs their Early Bird Sale where returners and new customers can sign up for a share for the following year at a discounted price.

Anyone can sign up at any time, even after the initial start date of the current year's shares. "Late" enrollees will receive the current month's box and afterwards.

TASTEABLE: How is this helping small businesses?

Sitka works closely with small-boat fishermen and we pay them fair and stable prices. We have a goal to deliver 15-20% more value than average dock prices. This gives our fishing fleet the support needed to focus on fishing like craftsmen, delivering the highest possible quality.

While not the traditional business one may think of when mentioning a small business, Sitka Salmon Shares

would not be here today without the fishermen families that have joined the company's CSF model and mission.

TASTEABLE: How does this improve the quality of the fish?

Most of the fish consumed in America is frozen once on shore, then shipped whole to a processor (often in China or Thailand), defrosted once it arrives so it can be filleted, and then refrozen and shipped back to the United States for sale.

At Sitka Salmon Shares, our wild seafood is caught in season and handled the moment it is fished from the waters. It is then iced, filleted and blast frozen to ensure a sashimi-grade quality for our subscribers. From there it is packaged and shipped to customers' doorsteps. The time spent getting seafood from the ocean to your doorstep is significantly less with Sitka Salmon Shares when compared to the fish being sold in your grocery store.

TASTEABLE: Is it just salmon?

Sitka Salmon Shares features seafood that is in season for their customers. Depending on the share, Sitka can provide wild Alaska king salmon, sockeye salmon, coho salmon, keta (chum) salmon, lingcod, black rockfish, sablefish (black cod), Pacific cod, yellow eye, rockfish, bairdi crab, Dungeness crab, albacore tuna, and halibut.

TASTEABLE: Some of your boxes often seem sold out. What are the most popular ones?

The most popular share is the Premium Sitka Seafood Share. It is our most bountiful share that includes all of the fish species included in the previous question. However, we do understand that signing up for a multi-month share is a large commitment.

Earlier this year, we launched our Freezer section. As with any service, we find we have a surplus of product after fulfilling our current shares. The company started to sell boxes highlighting our surplus. Anyone can go in to purchase a salmon sampler or any other seafood offered. These boxes are in limited quantities and reflect the season. Things like crab is a seafood favorite but only available during the winter months and will sell out faster than others. Once a supply is out it will not be restocked until it's fishing season comes around again in the following year.

TASTEABLE: What states are found to be most responsive?

Wisconsin, Illinois and Minnesota are the more responsive states. Sitka Salmon Shares is headquartered in Madison, WI and it was easier for the company to service these areas first. We had the benefit that these were also landlocked states where access to high quality seafood was not as available and it was through their word of mouth and enthusiasm that the company was able to expand to service subscribers in all the lower 48 states. With recent new growth and interest we are experiencing heightened interest from New York and Texas.

TASTEABLE: What is your biggest e-commerce challenge?

The logistics of getting premium fish from Sitka, Alaska to the front doors of houses across the country.

PORK WONTONS
GEORGE CHEN, CHINA LIVE
SAN FRANCISCO

WONTON INGREDIENTS:

1 Pound Ground Pork (preferred by Chinese but ground chicken, turkey or beef is fine)

1 Tb. Minced Ginger

2 Tb. Light Soy Sauce

1 Tb. Sesame Oil

1 Ts. Kosher Salt)

1 Ts. Sugar

1 Ts. Minced Garlic (optional

1 Eggwhite

2 Tb. Neutral Cooking Oil (Grapeseed, Avocado, Safflower are best)

1 Package Square Asian Wrappers (~14 Oz package - will not use all). At China Live, we make all our own wrappers, but that is not feasible for all home cooks.

DIPPING SAUCE INGREDIENTS (OPTIONAL):

1 Tb. Minced Ginger

2 Tb. Chopped Scallions (green and white parts)

2 Tb. Light Soy Sauce

1 Tb. Sesame Oil

1 Ts. Kosher Salt

1 Ts. Sugar

1 Ts. Minced Garlic

2 Tb. Rice Vinegar or Black Chiangkang Vinegar

EQUIPMENT:

Pot for Boiling

METHOD:

In a mixing bowl, mix in all Wontona ingredients excluding the Cooking Oil and Wrappers, and hand knead until mixture is like soft hamburger patty texture. Cover and set aside for 30 minutes.

With the square wrapper, place 1 tablespoon of the meat (half the potsticker amount) into the center, and dab the egg white mix on the 3 corners and press together. Here is the tricky part: to be fancy, you must twist the top flap corners onto the top flap of the opposite corner so they look like boats (or ancient Chinese gold ingots). But it is not necessary as you can bring them together as intuitively folding up the wings.

Cooking instructions vary but this is mostly a boiled dumpling. You can boil them in water or chicken stock, until they float and are transparent (do not overcook just like pasta). Use a slotted spoon to remove, add some sesame oil to the wontons to keep them from sticking if you are not having plain wonton soup. If for soup, boil the dumplings in water and make the soup on the side with whatever vegetables you like and then add the boiled wontons to the soup at the end because they all cook at different temperatures.

These wontons are delicious deep-fried as well. Fry gently in 325 Degree oil until golden brown, reserve over paper towels and serve with your favorite dipping sauce, can be same as for the potstickers or make a easy sweet and sour sauce or simply a aioli or savory fruit compote/chutney if that's what you prefer. The pork mixture can be lamb or chicken and even vegetarian but choose vegetables that are compatible as they need to cook consistently together into the wonton.

The optional dipping sauce is easy - just combine all the Sauce Ingredients including the vinegar and mix well. Let it sit for a while so make it in advance so the flavors are melted together. Add Chopped Cilantro if that is a herb you like, but this needs to be freshly added at the end.

CHAMPIONSHIP CHOCOLATE CHIP COOKIES

CHEF PHILLIP ASHLEY, PHILLIP ASHLEY CHOCOLATES
MEMPHIS

YIELD:

Makes 26 cookies

INGREDIENTS:

½ pound butter, softened (2 sticks)

1/2 cup granulated sugar

¾ cup packed light brown sugar

1/4 cup pure maple syrup

2 large eggs

¼ teaspoon freshly squeezed lemon juice

1/4 teaspoon cinnamon

2 ¼ cups flour

1 1/2 cup rolled oats

1 teaspoon baking soda

1 teaspoon salt

1 1/2 cups dark chocolate chunks

1 1/2 cups milk chocolate chunks

1 1/2 cups chopped pecans

1 cup fine chopped thick cut bacon

METHOD:

Cream butter, sugar and brown sugar in the bowl of a stand mixer on medium speed for about 2 minutes.

Add eggs, maple syrup and lemon juice, blending with mixer on low speed for 30 seconds, then medium speed for about 2 minutes, or until light and fluffy, scraping down bowl.

With mixer on low speed, add flour, baking soda, salt and cinnamon, blending for about 45 seconds. Don't over mix.

Remove bowl from mixer and fold in oats chocolate chunks bacon and pecans.

Portion dough with a scoop (about 3 tablespoons) onto a baking sheet lined with parchment paper about 2 inches apart.

Preheat oven to 300°F. Bake for 20 to 23 minutes, or until edges are golden brown and center is still soft.

Remove from oven and cool on baking sheet for about 1 hour.

Note: You can freeze the unbaked cookies, and there's no need to thaw. Preheat oven to 300°F and place frozen cookies on parchment paper-lined baking sheet about 2 inches apart. Bake until edges are golden brown and center is still soft.

Above: Chocolate creations and ingredients from Phillip Ashley Rix, Founder & CEO of Phillip Ashley Chocolates: Woodford Reserve Double Oaked Bourbon, French Bleu Cheese, Cherry Pomegranate Molasses. www.phillipashleychocolates.com

EASY **RACK OF LAMB**

TASTE TV NETWORKS

Sometimes you can overdo the recipe for a great piece of meat, especially one that is as delicious as a cut of Aussie lamb. That is why this TasteTV Kitchen's recipe only relies on a handful of ingredients and prep.

Although we are huge fans of American lamb, we cannot walk away from a tasty source like Australia. Australia is known for many culinary treats, and one of them is great lamb. Aussie grass fed beef and lamb is healthier than some other sources and types of meats, and is very time efficient to cook, often reducing meal prep time by 30%.

Australia ranchers also have made a large effort to be more sustainable. In a study over the last 30 years, Aussie ranchers have:

- Reduced their water use by over 65%
- Reduced their animals' greenhouse gas emissions intensity by 14%

It doesn't make the meat taste better, but it definitely helps satisfy your soul.

METHOD:

Combine the olive oil with salt pepper, garlic powder, and herbs in a bowl. Mix well.

Score the fatty side of the rack of lamb in a cross-hatch formation with a sharp knife

Using a spoon or brush, spread the olive oil mixture over both sides of the meat evenly and allow to marinate for 15 minutes to an hour

Heat oven to 450°

Place rack of lamb with fatty side up on a baking tray covered with aluminum foil or parchment paper.

Roast for 30 minutes

Remove from oven, allowed to rest for 10 minutes. Slice and serve

INGREDIENTS:

1 Rack of Lamb

3 Tablespoons of extra virgin olive oil

2 teaspoons of kosher or sea salt

2 teaspoons of garlic powder

1 teaspoon of Oregano (dried or fresh)

1 teaspoon of Rosemary or Thyme (dried or fresh)
   Pepper to taste

DUNGENESS CRAB CAKES

MCCORMICK AND KULETO'S SEAFOOD RESTAURANT

SAN FRANCISCO

"There are as many recipes for crab cakes as there are chefs. This one takes the straightforward approach, whisk we think is best. Try not to break up the crab meat too much while you're mixing. The texture will be better if the crab is chunky."

YIELD:

Makes 8 cakes. 3 1/2" in diameter, or 30-40 mini-cakes for hors d'oeuvres.

INGREDIENTS:

1 1/2 Lb crab meat, cleared of shell fragments

1 cup plain bread crumbs

2 celery stalks, finely minced

1 small onion, finely minced

1 small green pepper, finely minced

1 tsp dry mustard

1/2 tsp Tabasco

1 large egg

1/4 cup mayonnaise

1 Tbs Worcestershire sauce

Additional bread crumbs for coating the crab cakes

1/2 cup oil for frying (or more)

1 cup jalapeno hollandaise (see below)

Hollandaise Sauce, Makes about 1 1/2 cup

1/2 Lb unsalted butter, melted and warm, but not hot

3 egg yolks

1 Tbs water

1 Tbs lemon juice

Pinch salt

METHOD:

Hollandaise Sauce:

Melt the butter and reserve. Combine the egg yolks and water in the top of a double boiler over hot, but not boiling water and stir briskly with a wire whisk until the mixture is light and fluffy and the consistency of light mayonnaise. Remove the tip of the double boiler from the heat and slowly add the butter in a thin stream, while continuing to whip the mixture. Season the mixture with the lemon juice and salt to taste.

Crab Cakes:

Preheat oven to 200 degrees Fahrenheit. Combine all the ingredients except the bread crumbs for coating, the oil for frying and the tartar sauce. Form the mixture into eight 3 inch to 3 1/2 inches by 1 inch thick crab cakes, or 30 to 40 mini-cakes for hors d'oeuvres. Coat cakes on both sides with the additional bread crumbs, patting the crumbs lightly into cakes. If you are making large cakes, put about 1/4 cup oil into a 10" to 12" saute pan and cook over medium heat. Cook 4 cakes at a time, 4 minutes per side. They should be nicely browned on both sides and heated through. Keep the 4 cooked cakes warm in the oven while you prepare the remaining 4. Use fresh oil for the second batch. If you're making mini cakes, put the entire 1/2 cup oil in the saute pan and fry 10 to 15 at a time, turning once until dark brown. You may need to replace the oil once between batches of mini cakes. Keep cooked mini cakes warm in oven while you cook the rest.

SMOKED TROUT POTATO CAKE WITH CREME FRAICHE & SALMON ROE

CHEF DEBBIE GOLD, BRAVO TV

Debbie Gold, Bravo TV Top Chef Master and James Beard Awarded Chef shares her recipe for Smoked Trout Potato Cake with Crème Fraiche and Salmon Roe

INGREDIENTS:

4 ounces Smoked Trout

2 tablespoons Crème fraiche

2 ounces Salmon Roe

For the Potato Cake

1 pound russet potatoes (about 3 potatoes)

1/2 medium yellow onion, peeled

1 clove garlic, minced

1 teaspoon kosher salt

1/8 teaspoon freshly ground pepper

1 to 1 ½ cups canola oil

2 pieces of chive, cut into 1 inch long pieces

METHOD:

Heat the oven to 350*F. Arrange a rack in the middle of the oven. Fit one baking sheet with paper towels and another with a cooling rack. Scrub the potatoes well, but do not peel. Grate potatoes on a large holed square box grater. Then grate the onion. Place the potato and onion in a medium mixing bowl. Add the garlic, salt and pepper. Toss al the ingredients together. Heat the oil in a large heavy bottomed skillet (like a cast iron pan) so that there is a depth of ¼ inch. Heat over medium high heat until a piece of potato sizzles immediately. Heap about ¼ cup of potato-onion mixture onto the hot oil. Continue until you use up all the potato mixture. Let the potato cakes cook about 4-5 minutes until they are golden brown on each side. Remove the potato cakes and place on the paper towels. Then place on the cooling rack tray and put them in the oven for 5 minutes, to be sure the interior of the potato cake is cooked through.

PLATING:

Place the potato cakes in the middle of a plate. Put a small dollop of crème fraiche on top of each potato cake. Decoratively place a piece of smoked trout so it rests on the crème fraiche. Garnish with a half an ounce of salmon roe and then some chives

GRILLED TAJIN & MAPLE CHICKEN WINGS

CHEF DENNIS PRESCOTT, NETFLIX

A once struggling musician living in Nashville, Dennis Prescott is now a celebrated Canadian chef and cookbook author, with almost 600,000 Instagram followers. His bestselling cookbook, Eat Delicious: 125 Recipes For Your Daily Dose of Awesome was published in 2017. Currently he is the resident chef of Netflix's series, "Restaurants on the Edge." For this season, Chef Prescott has created a delicious recipe for Grilled Tajín & Maple Chicken Wings.

INGREDIENTS:

For the Chicken Wings

2 pounds chicken wings

1 tablespoon olive oil

2 teaspoons Tajín

Glaze & Garnish

¼ cup pure maple syrup

3 tablespoons fresh squeezed lime juice

1 teaspoon Tajín

To Serve

¼ cup minced cilantro leaves, to garnish

Extra lime wedges, to serve

METHOD:

When ready to cook, preheat a grill to medium-high heat.

In a large bowl, combine wings, olive oil, Tajin, and toss until the chicken is completely coated in the mixture. (Note! This step can be done up to 4 hours before grilling – the longer the wings marinate in the Tajín mixture, the better.)

Transfer the wings to the grill, placing directly on the grill grates in a single layer. Cook for 15 – 20 minutes, turning halfway through, until golden on the outside and cooked through on the inside (and the chicken has reached an internal temperature of 165 degrees F).

Meanwhile, combine maple, lime, and Tajín in a large bowl and mix well. When the chicken wings are done, immediately transfer them to the maple glaze bowl and toss well to coat entirely in glaze.

Transfer chicken wings to a serving platter and sprinkle over the cilantro. Serve immediately with extra lime wedges.

BLUEBERRY CHEESECAKE ICE CREAM BARS

MICHELLE HARRIS, ALIVE & WELL TV

Blueberry cheesecake is a decadent dessert staple. I wanted to make this classic dessert a bit healthier, so I made it plant-based and frozen. Now it's lighter, better for you, and freezing it adds a refreshing twist. I also added Sambucol black elderberry syrup to the sauce for a great immune boost!

INGREDIENTS:

1 cup frozen blueberries

¼ cup raw coconut sugar

1 package plant-based frozen cream cheese

1 pint non-dairy vanilla ice cream (I use So Delicious cashew based ice-cream for a great creamy texture and taste)

2 TBS agave syrup

4 TBS Sambucol Black Elderberry syrup

Fresh blueberries for garnish

Non-dairy whipped topping

METHOD:

Allow frozen blueberries to reach room temperature. Heat on low in a saucepan and add coconut sugar. Stir until mixture bubbles and allow to cool.

Set out cream cheese and frozen dessert for 10-15 minutes to soften.

Once cream cheese is soft, cream in agave, then add vanilla frozen non-dairy ice cream dessert. Add in half of cooled blueberry mixture and Sambucol Black Elderberry Syrup.

Stir until well mixed and add to a container (for bars use a rectangular container) which can be frozen.

Place in freezer to set overnight.

Place the remainder of the blueberry mixture in the refrigerator.

Once frozen, cut into bars. Serve with a small amount of the blueberry mixture on top and a spoonful of non-dairy whipped topping. Garnish with fresh blueberries.
Dig in and enjoy a yummy treat that you can feel good about!

A CAKE TO DIE FOR: FLOURLESS CHOCOLATE CAKE

JANET RUDOLPH, FOOD WRITER

This is a great dense delicious flourless cake.

INGREDIENTS:

1 pound 4 ounces bittersweet chocolate, chopped

12 ounces unsalted butter

18 egg yolks

4 ounces granulated sugar

3 ounces cocoa powder

METHOD:

Preheat oven to 325F. Butter and flour 10 inch round baking pan. Line bottom with parchment paper.

In double boiler or pot over pot over simmering water, melt chocolate with butter. Cool slightly. In stand mixer, whip egg yolks with sugar until very light, about 5 minutes.

Fold cooled chocolate mixture into egg sugar mixture. Sift in cocoa powder.

On medium speed, beat mixture just to combine. Mixture will appear fudgy and heavy.

Transfer to prepared pan and bake in water bath for 25 minutes.

Sift more cocoa powder or confectioner's sugar on top of cake to serve.

LOOKING FOR **NATURAL HONEY**

TRY THESE 3 FAMILY-OWNED BRANDS FROM CALIFORNIA

Most honey is good for you, but the kind that comes from small family-owned producers is often the healthiest, and the tastiest. California is world renowned as being an excellent source of artisan honey. It is also one of the largest honey producing states, right Behind North Dakota and often ahead of Montana, South Dakota and Texas. Each year California produces almost 14,000 Pounds of Honey. In fact, for this reason as well as sustainability, all bees are considered valuable that in California even wild native bumble bees may become protected under the California's Endangered Species Act.

We've tried many honey producers from the Golden State, and here are three family-owned brands you should try right now:
3 FAMILY-OWNED CALIFORNIA HONEYS

TRUE GOLD HONEY

True Gold is owned by mother-son duo Sarah and Tyler Sample, both of whom are 3rd and 4th generation beekeepers. They've grown up in the apiary business, and know their way around the hives with skills and experience. Their bee farm is called the Sample Family Apiaries, with their separate honey business called True Gold.

ORANGE BLOSSOMEZ HONEY & WILDFLOWER HONEY

The True Gold Orange Blossom honey is a golden color with a citrus element of course, plus some zest. The Samples say that it can only be harvested where the weather is mild enough for orange trees to survive. Fortunately, the trees for their orange blossom honey basically come from around their own homes.

True Gold is well recognized for excellence, and has won Good Food Awards, Cal Expo Awards, and others.

https://truegoldhoney.com

KISS THE FLOWER HONEY

Kiss the Flower Honey Company was founded in 2010, and focuses on best practices for bees, people, and the planet. They use only natural methods, and have several hives in Sonoma County, including a Santa Rosa property, as well as in the West County. The flowers used in the honey include eucalyptus, Himalayan Blackberry, apples, and acacias. Kiss the Flower produces only about 3,000 pounds of honey per year.

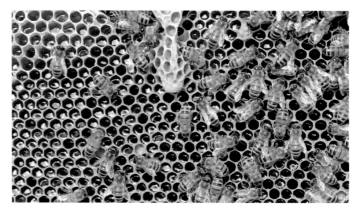

WILDLFLOWER HONEY

The Kiss the Flower Wildflower is classic honey. Their wildflower honey comes from hives on Mount Taylor in Santa Rosa.

STARTHISTLE HONEY

The Kiss the Flower Starthistle honey is a light gold color, with a mild and flowery flavor profile, as well as a bit of anise and cinnamon.

https://kisstheflowerhoney.com

SEKA HILLS HONEY

Seka Hills has a line of tribal products that honor Northern California's Capay Valley. The Native Tribe is known as the Yocha Dehe Wintun Nation
meaning 'Home by the Spring Water.' In the native Patwin language, 'Séka' means 'blue.'

The Tribe's product decisions are based on good environmental stewardship, with over 22,000 total acres in production in Yolo County

WILDFLOWER HONEY

The Seka Hills Wildflower Honey gets its taste and dark amber color from variety of wildflowers, such as redbud, rose clover and ceanothus, which are found on over 9,000 acres of tribal land. They produce the artisan honey in partnership with beekeeper John Foster

https://www.sekahills.com/

HOT UKRAINIAN BORSCHT

EMMA KRASOV, ART & ENTERTAIN ME

INGREDIENTS:

40 oz chicken broth or 1 box and a quarter of store-bought chicken stock or broth

1 large onion

2 carrots

2-3 medium red beets

1 medium green cabbage

1 large potato

1 parsnip root (optional)

2-3 tablespoons of tomato paste, or half cup of tomato sauce, or 1 cup of tomato juice

Lemon juice of half-lemon

Fresh dill or parsley

Salt and pepper to taste

Sour cream for serving

Rye bread for serving

METHOD:

Pour chicken broth into a large pot.

Bring to boil and lower the flame to medium
Add to lightly boiling broth chopped onion, sliced carrots and whole beets. Cook on medium for 15 minutes.

Add diced potato, and cook for another 15 min
Take out beets with slotted spoon and let them cool.

Add shredded cabbage to the pot. Cook for 10-15 min. until soft, but not mushy.

Add tomato paste and stir well so it'll dissolve. If adding tomato sauce or tomato juice, don't add it just yet
Grate cooled beets on a big-hole grater or just slice thinly. Sprinkle with lemon juice to retain color. Add to the pot.

Add tomato sauce or juice (if not using tomato paste).

Add salt and pepper, stir.

Let it cook on low heat for a couple of minutes.

Taste and adjust seasoning. Can add hot pepper flakes, paprika, cayenne, more lemon juice, and practically any dried herbs, but in small amounts, to taste.

Turn off heat, add chopped fresh dill or parsley, and cover with lid for a minute.

SERVING:

Put a spoonful of sour cream in each bowl.

Serve hot with a slice of rye bread and an optional raw garlic clove.

Refrigerate leftovers and enjoy even more on day 2 and 3.

Keeps well for 5-7 days, and only improves with time.

San Francisco journalist Emma Krasov writes about art, food, and travel. She also writes for Russian-language newspapers published in San Francisco, Chicago, and Detroit, and for an array of English-language publications, including her own popular award-winning blog, Art and Entertain Me.

REAL OYSTER CULT

LIVE OYSTERS DELIVERED STRAIGHT TO YOUR DOORSTEP

Fresh oysters are a delicacy that require one main ingredient, and that's freshness. So when we heard about seafood company **Real Oyster Cult**, that says they will deliver fresh oysters across the country to you, and guarantees that they are actually fresh, we had to take a look at it. Fortunately, we found that this promise was in fact delivered upon 100%.

The oysters that we received were all tightly closed within their shells, proof that they were not only alive but also determined to remain that way, with their freshness and sea water inside. Not a single one had even the slightest hint of an open shell. The overall reviewers' verdict on their taste was an A+.

Real Oyster Cult is one of several national or local firms that have moved into the area of bringing sustainably harvested seafood directly to people's homes. These oysters arrive live in an insulated cold storage device, which allows them to be stored in a home refrigerator for up to 10 days without a problem.

Of course, who is really going to keep live oysters in the refrigerator for 10 days without eating them? But it's good to know that you have the option, as long as you keep them on ice.

Real Oyster Cult says that this entire idea came to them because they are already oyster farmers, and they were in the habit of throwing great parties on their floating workspace above the oyster beds, a perfect place to concoct this new business model.

Seems like they did a great job with that idea. Not only do they send the oysters that they cultivate themselves, they also now include the opportunity for seafood lovers to taste oysters from over 70 different farms from across North America. The 20 oysters that we received in the Real Oyster Cult Gift Bundle package were of three different types, and this was from a possible curated selection of over 20 varieties oysters available. The package can be increased by 20 oysters at a time, and they can send a bundle of 40 or 60 oysters, depending on your needs. The Gift Bundle also includes a free shucking knife and rubberized non-slip gloves, which are not just practical and safe, but also a delight to use. They definitely speed up the process if you don't have an oyster knife and gloves already available. If you don't eat oysters on a regular basis, the gloves can alternately be used in the garden.

On top of being a tasty luxury, oysters are known for having multiple health and wellness benefits. Furthermore, apparently being an oyster farmer is more than a delicious occupation, although tiring. It also helps keep the natural environment clean. Oysters clean the ocean and can filter nitrogen from 25 to 50 gallons of sea water every day. Too much nitrogen is not good for the ecosystem, and oysters contribute to keeping it balanced. Real Oyster Cult says that helping to support this balance is part of their overall mission.

In addition to the several varieties of oysters available, Real Oyster Cult also has seasoning sauces and hot sauces (called Mignon-Nips), wine and whiskey pairing packages, caviar, Maine Lobster, and Jonah Crab Claws. The Gift Bundle starts at around $69.

www.realoystercult.com

JUICY DUCK BREAST IN RED WINE SAUCE

TASTE TV NETWORKS

In some parts of the world duck is a regular dish, especially among people who hunt it. But if you're not a hunter or don't live in those areas then duck might be a little bit more uncommon on your table. We recently have been testing recipes with **Maple Leaf Farms** duck breast, which is well known for some of the highest quality duck selections in the United States. Not to mention being a fairly upscale red meat option, the duck meat itself is quite lean and tasty.

When you cook duck breast for the first few times it's best not to be too fancy, especially when you have the savory natural flavors already inherent in this type of poultry. We prefer to start off with a simple salt, pepper, garlic powder and skillet or oven recipe.

For example, using a sharp knife you score crosswise the fatty side of the duck. Then salt, pepper, and lightly powder both sides, and place the fatty side face down in a hot skillet with a small amount of California olive oil for about 10 minutes while the fat is rendering. Flip over and cook the other side for another 5 to 10 minutes on medium high. Alternatively, you could heat your oven to 425° and put the uncooked breast in for 10 minutes, then flip it to cook for another 10 minutes. It's important to let your breast rest after you remove it from the skillet or oven so that it can re-absorb some of those juices and remain tender.

After you remove the duck from the skillet or pan, put the skillet back on the stove and heat to medium high and add a large splash of red wine, which you can use to create a red wine reduction sauce. You want to make sure that you use a spoon to scrape up the bits of fat and duck in the skillet and mix them into the sauce reduction. You also want to make sure the sauce has thickened and all of the alcohol in the wine has evaporated before using.

This sauce is perfect for the duck breast as it adds additional moisture and flavor, plus is a perfect complement to this dish.

It doesn't have to be fancy, but it's not going to be boring and plain.

www.MapleLeafFarms.com

Un soir, l'âme du vin chantait dans les bouteilles :

" Homme, vers toi je pousse, ô cher déshérité,

Sous ma prison de verre et mes cires vermeilles,

Un chant plein de lumière et de fraternité !"

L'âme du vin
(*The Soul of Wine*)

Charles BAUDELAIRE (1821-1867)

One night, the soul of wine was singing in the bottles:
"O man, dear disinherited, to you I sing
From my prison of glass with its scarlet wax seals.
This song full of light and of brotherhood!"

WHITE & DESSERT WINES:
EDITORS CHOICE

IN ORDER, LEFT TO RIGHT:

Weinstock Cellar Select 2018 Clarksburg Chardonnay

Parducci 2019 Small Lot Mendocino County Chardonnay

Ferrari-Carano 2008 Villa Fiore Fior di Moscato Muscat

Casteller Cava Rosé Brut, Sant Sadurni d'Anoia, Spain

Herzog 2016 Late Harvest California Orange Muscat

R&B Cellars The Improviser, Vintner's White Blend

Sangiacomo 2018 Sonoma Cosat Chardonnay

RED WINES: EDITORS CHOICE

13 can be a Lucky Number, and we believe that these 13 California red wines are going to be lucky for you.

These wines are some of our favorites, well balanced and with a lot of variety. Each has been created by a family owned organization, and led by diverse winemakers with skill, expertise, and passion. It shows in the vintages, and you will feel it in the glass.

ABOVE: San Simeon 2018 Cabernet Sauvignon, Paso Robles. Windstream 2018 Pinot Noir, Sarmento Vineyard.

BELOW: Parrish 2017 Estate Cabernet Sauvignon, Paso Robles. Parrish 2017 Silken, Paso Robles. Anaba 2018 Pinot Noir, Sonoma Coast.

ABOVE: Mira 2016 Cabernet Sauvignon, Yountville Napa Valley. Mira 2017 Jimmy D's Red Blend. Lava Cap 2019 Cabernet Sauvignon, Sierra Foothills. Lava Cap Mourvedre, Sierra Foothills.

BELOW: Trefethen 2018 Cabernet Sauvignon, Estate Grown, Oak Knoll. Trefethen 2018 Dragon's Tooth Napa Valley Red Wine. Broadside 2019 Cabernet Sauvignon, Margarita Vineyard. Broadside 2018 Blackletter Cabernet Sauvignon, Paso Robles.

COLLECTORS REPORT:
WINE TRAVELERS GALLERY

Often to discover a good bottle of wine you have to go to other places and have them presented to you by the sommelier, winemaker, or a trusted friend. In other words, you don't discover the wines, they discover you.

Here are a few that we discovered, as writer Jack Kerouac would say, "on the road."

Ackerman Family Vineyards

2014 Le Chatelaine, Napa Valley

Vina Robles

2012 Petit Verdot, Huerhuero Vineyard, Paso Robles

Coho Wines

2017 Pinot Noir, Stanly Ranch, Los Carneros

Poseidon Vineyards

2015 Pinot Noir, Estate Grown, Caneros, Napa Valley

Thumbprint Cellars

2015 "Redacted" Red Blend, Sonoma County

DOMAINE DE TASTE: THE GIFT

This boutique wine was developed by R&B for TasteTV and the Awards as a reflection of America's heritage grape. The base of this blend is Zinfandel from the Del Barba and Favalora Vineyards in Contra Costa county. Both vineyards are over 25 years old and are a combination of trellised and head trained vines. Contra Costa fruit often yields one of the most classic expressions of Zinfandel: red cherries, hints of plum, and a little spiciness. Married together with Petite Sirah from both Napa Valley and Lake County and a touch of Lake County Mourvedre, it was aged in a combination of French and American oak. This Zin blend is luscious and mouth filling. It can be matched with a myriad of dishes such as roast, burgers, lamb, goose, dark chocolate, or even portabella mushrooms. The wine was lovingly made by R&B Cellars for TasteTV. www.DomaineDeTaste.com

ANABA WINES:
JOHN T. SWEAZEY AND JOHN MICHAEL SWEAZEY

In addition to the new wine vintages, Anaba recently opened their new Anaba Vintners House in October, 2019. It is a reflection of the Sweazey family's belief in gracious and uncomplicated hospitality. Broad windows look out over the estate vineyards, drawing the eye to the distant hills, while private seating areas allow for leisurely personalized wine exploration. The color palette takes inspiration from nature – evoking fog, water, earth and even the Anabatic winds that give the winery its name. Beyond the landscaped courtyard, paddle tennis and bocce ball offer an unexpected chance to engage in a bit of competition. We talk with General Manager John Michael Sweazey to find out a bit more about this winery, and why they admire their Chardonnays and Pinot Noirs.

Winery Name: Anaba Wines
Owner: John T. Sweazey and John Michael Sweazey
Winemaker(s): Katy Wilson
Established: 2009

TASTE: Why did you decide to make your Pinots in this style?

John Michael Sweazey: It's hard to describe our wine as any one particular style. Originally, we were inspired by the red wines of Burgundy in the early 70s. But, we are not in Burgundy, and we can't make Burgundian Pinot. Instead, we make a number of different Sonoma Pinots, and the aim is always to let the fruit speak for itself. For the Sonoma Coast Pinot in particular, the goal was universal appeal. From first-time wine tasters to certified sommeliers, we wanted to make a well-integrated wine that was indicative of what the Sonoma Coast should be.

TASTE: Are there any elements of terroir that the drinker of your Pinot Noir should notice?

John Michael Sweazey: Yes, showcasing the terroir is a priority, and so there are many different elements. For the Sonoma Coast Pinot, you will notice a lot of red, bright fruit notes that are common to the AVA. The wine has the energy and vibrancy one would expect from a classic Pinot made in Sonoma.

TASTE: What are the most noticeable elements in your Chardonnay?

John Michael Sweazey: For our Sonoma Coast Chardonnay, the wet stone/flint and minerality, accompanied by citrus and stone fruit notes show through and are an expression of the land from which the fruit is sourced.

TASTE: What is the inspiration for your newest wine releases?

John Michael Sweazey: Our WestLands Chardonnay comes mostly from a higher elevation vineyard, located in northwest Sonoma and very close to the coast. The cooler climate shares some commonalities with northern Burgundy, and if we had to choose one place as the inspiration, it would be Chablis. The wine is nuanced, with depth from a touch new oak and the grape itself, but the high acid levels keep it crisp. Also, it is distinct from the wines of Chablis, but it is our representation of the possibilities of the fruit grown in the western-most parts of Sonoma Coast.

TASTE: What are the most exciting attributes about these wines?

John Michael Sweazey: In short, you might notice the subtle oak expression. Or that one can enjoy upon release, but can also let the wines age for several years. This is a hard balance to obtain. They can also pair with many foods, or can be enjoyed alone.

TASTE: With which foods do you recommend this pairs?

John Michael Sweazey: Pork or duck with the Pinot. Halibut, oysters, chicken with the Chardonnay.

TASTE: What's next for Anaba Wines?

John Michael Sweazey: We are planning to plant Picpoul Blanc at our property, and we are working with three new vineyards throughout Sonoma to produce a number of Rhone varieties.

TasteTV WINE RATINGS

- 4.00 out of 5 Stars: 2017 Sonoma Coast Chardonnay
- 4.25 out of 5 Stars: 2017 Sonoma Coast Pinot Noir

Find them at www.anabawines.com

BROADSIDE WINES:
ANNA FRIZZELL

You may be familiar with the instantly recognizable Broadside Wine label designs, as well as their reliably delicious flavors. We talk with Anna of Wine Hooligans to find out a bit more about this winery, and why she admires the Broadside Chardonnay & Cabernets.

Winery Name: Broadside
Owner: Wine Hooligans LLC
Winemaker(s): Adam LaZarre, Director of Winemaking; Brian Terrizzi, Winemaker for Blackletter Cabernet
Established: 2006

TASTE: Hi Anna, you have a lot of wines from which to choose, why are these your wine picks to spotlight in our interview?

I thought the Broadside 2018 Margarita Vineyard Cabernet would be a great selection for dads. It's a single vineyard Cabernet for less than $25 and is amazingly rich and bold for the money.

And, for those looking for something even more special, the Broadside Blackletter Cabernet is just that. It all starts in the vineyard with hand-picked fruit coming from a hillside vineyard called Grosso Kresser and select blocks from the Margarita Vineyard. Further hand-selections are made at the winery during crush, followed by a slow fermentation with native yeasts present on the grapes themselves and ambient strains living in the winery. The final lots spent over 20 months in French oak barrels before final blending. This is a very special bottle with only 900 cases produced.

TASTE: What are the most exciting attributes about these wines?

Well, in addition to the above, the Broadside 2018 Chardonnay recently made it onto Food & Wine's list of 12 Excellent Affordable Wines to Buy Right Now.

We also picked up a 90 point score from Vinous on this vintage.

TASTE: Congratulations on those high points!

The Margarita Vineyard is an amazingly special place at the southernmost tip of Paso Robles. Vineyards are located on a working ranch in the Santa Margarita Ranch AVA and sit amongst ancient oaks, with incredible bio and geological diversity. Vineyards were first planted in 1999 and are SIP certified (one of the strictest standards for environmental protection).

TASTE: The Chardonnay is very much what you want in that varietal, and does not disappoint. Our wine tasters particularly enjoyed the melange of ripe blackberry, smoky leather and subtle tobacco elements in the Broadside 2018 Margarita Vineyard Cabernet. Are there any elements of terroir in these wines that the drinker should notice?

Absolutely. The terroir of Paso Robles contributes greatly to the excellence of our wines. [There is a lot of research] dedicated to talking about the soils and terroir of Paso for your reference.

TASTE: The Broadside wines can absolutely be enjoyed on their own, but of course we often like to have something delicious to eat. With which foods do you recommend these pair, Anna?

I'd recommend a spring pasta for the Broadside 2018 Chardonnay. Something like rigatoni with English peas, carrots, green garlic and toasted walnuts. The Broadside 2018 Margarita Cabernet goes will with BBQ pork—something really juicy and delicious. The Broadside 2018 Blackletter Cabernet has more structure, but still has a sense of lushness and I think pairs really well with seared filet mignon or a mushroom fettuccini.

TasteTV WINE RATINGS

- 3.75 out of 5 Stars: Broadside 2018 Central Coast Chardonnay – $17.99 SRP
- 4 out of 5 Stars: Broadside 2018 Margarita Vineyard Cabernet – $23.99 SRP
- 4.3 out of 5 Stars: Broadside Blackletter 2017 Paso Robles Cabernet – $79.99 SRP

Find them at www.Broadsidewine.com

UNION WINE COMPANY: RYAN HARMS

Canned wines continue to grow as a hot product category that people more and more want to discover, and to drink. Union Wine Company is the group behind the Underwood line of canned wines, which was one of the earliest successful pioneers in bringing canned wines to stores across the world. Union was able to beat several of the challenges involving canned wine, such as creating the right packaging, eliminating various elements that can affect the taste of the wine in cans, and of course, changing consumer perspectives on canned wine's quality.

It is very likely that you have already seen Underwood's Pinot Noir and Pinot Gris in the wine section of your local grocery. If you haven't tried their new line of flavored wines, such as the Mei Wine and the Strawberry Cooler, then definitely add those to your list. Our tasters were quite pleased with them, especially when you are looking for something light and unique.

We speak with Ryan Harms, founder and owner of the Union Wine Company, and Joan Olbrantz, marketing operations manager, on what they did right, and why you will love their vintages.

Winery Name: Union Wine Company
Owner: Ryan Harms
Winemaker(s): JP Caldcleugh
Established: 2005

TASTE: Canned wine has a very high growth rate. Why is it becoming so popular?

Ryan Harms: From a business standpoint, canned wine is a popular choice because it costs approximately 40% less to package compared to the equivalent 9 liter case of wine in glass bottles. Putting wine in a can opens up the wine drinking experience to places where it had previously been difficult, such as outdoor events or when portability is needed. People are certainly seeing the lifestyle applications for the cans in their lives. The outdoor and active sport community has certainly embraced the cans, and we are also seeing folks in big cities purchase them for the portion size for home or outings around town.

From a consumer standpoint, we think this is a timing thing, culturally. There was a "winification" of beer trend going on with the craft beer craze, and we're at the forefront of a new trend: the "beerification" of wine. Consumers are signaling an acceptance and we believe they are demanding brands to be innovative to connect to their needs. The eco-elements of the can are appealing and culturally relevant as well.

TASTE: You have your own proprietary tech for canning wine. What makes it different?

Ryan Harms: Union Wine Company has the fastest and most automated bottling and canning facility in Oregon. California has faster more sophisticated production facilities, but there's nothing like this in Oregon, especially for wine. From a canning perspective, this facility is unprecedented in the canned wine industry.

TASTE: What is the inspiration for your newest wine releases, esp. the fruit flavors?

Ryan Harms: We look at our wine coolers as alternatives to both wine or beer. We don't see this as an either/or proposition, rather, a traditional beer drinker might like an alternative on a warm sunny day, and same with a wine drinker – looking for something a bit more crisp and refreshing (with less alcohol content).

The Riesling Radler is our own spin on the traditional beer beverage that includes a refreshing blend of Oregon Riesling, hops and grapefruit.

The Strawberry Cooler is a fresh take on a retro classic wine cooler. We make it with the same great Underwood Pinot Noir we put in our bottles, a splash of fresh strawberries and a hint of lime.

Mei Wine is a product collaboration with Chef Mei Lin. Mei is the Season 12 winner of Bravo TV's Top Chef, and we worked with her to blend her signature culinary flavors into our wine to create a tropical, bold-yet-reassuring wine cooler.

TASTE: What the most exciting attributes about these wines?

Ryan Harms: Union Wine Company (and the Underwood brand) was created to bring great, affordable Oregon wines to everyone, not just one audience in particular. Whether they're a seasoned wine enthusiast or a beer drinker just now entering the world of wine – Underwood cans make it approachable, accessible and fun. For instance, Underwood wine in a can is ideal for the adventurer, as a way to bring wine outdoors without the weight. However, the single-serving option the can provides is also convenient for a night in as the perfect solution for consumers who don't want to commit to opening an entire bottle. Each can is equivalent to half a bottle of wine which makes it easy to enjoy on your own or share.

TASTE: Are there any elements of terroir that the drinker of your Pinot Noir and Gris should notice?

Joan Olbrantz: Underwood Pinot Noir and Pinot Gris are Oregon wines, made with Oregon grapes. That all by itself is noteworthy as Oregon produces some of the best Pinot grapes in the world.

TASTE: How is business being affected by COVID?

Joan Olbrantz: Our online business is doing well during this time as could be expected. We also aren't as heavy into on premise sales as we are at regular retail, so that has been an advantage for us during this time as well.

Find them at www.unionwinecompany.com/

JERKY & SNACKS: EDITORS CHOICE

Jamie's Jerky, Jamie's Jerky Original Beef

The world is full of fantastic, delicious, and innovative jerky and healthy snacks. That's why our panel of experts tastes each year some of the best, and ranks and celebrates what they find.

There is no reason to sacrifice either taste or quality when you have some of these fantastic choices to try.

Matt-Hat Jerky Gourmet Keto Original

Jedsjerky Tropical Sweet & Spicy Mango Brisket

Eat The Change Eat The Change Mushroom Jerky

Healthy Oceans Seafood Company Pescavore Ahi Tuna Jerky Strip Caribbean Jerk

Fat Cow Jerky Honey Habanero Beef Jerky

Neptune Snacks Spicy Cajun Wild Pacific Rockfish Jerky

The Good Jerky Sweet Honey Teriyaki Salmon Jerky

Smoke Shack Jerky dojo Mojo Beef Jerky

Pollard's Gentleman Jerky Oklahoma Blend Medium Heat

Savage Jerky Co. Maple Buffalo Bacon Jerky

Bella Sun Luci The Original Plant-Based Tomato Jerky Teriyaki and Cracked Pepper

Homefree "Treats You Can Trust" Lemon Burst Cookies

Clio Strawberry Greek Yogurt Bar

Alskinny Bros Health Foods Pumpkin Granola

88 Acres Dark Chocolate Sea Salt Seed Bar

88 Acres Cinnamon & Oats Seed'nola

Three Dads Superfood Popcorn

Wai Lana Rice Chips : Nacho Cheese (Vegan)

Airly Foods Oat Clouds Snack Crackers with Sea Salt

LOVE CORN Smoked BBQ

88 Acres Dark Chocolate Sunflower Seed Butter

Wai Lana Rice Chips : Sour Cream & Chives (Vegan)

THE CHOCOLATE REPORT

BEST CHOCOLATIERS AND CONFECTIONERS IN AMERICA

Looking for the best chocolate in America? You are in luck. TasteTV and the International Chocolate Salon recently announced the 2021 award winners for the title BEST CHOCOLATIERS AND CONFECTIONERS IN AMERICA.

The Best Chocolatiers and Confectioners in America Award winners are based on the combined total number of Gold and Silver Awards and plus 4.5/4.0/3.5 star ratings received by each entrant in the in the previous year's TasteTV Chocolate Salons in San Francisco, Los Angeles, Sacramento, and Fall (SF), as well as in the standalone International Chocolate Salon Award Competitions for Best Caramels, Toffees, Bars, Truffles, White Chocolate, Best Hot Cocoa and Drinking Chocolate, Vegan Chocolates, Spicy Chocolates, and Best Valentine's Chocolates. For more information about the Artisan Chocolate Awards and the ICS, visit www.internationalchocolatesalon.com

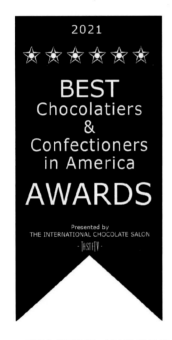

SIX STAR AWARDS

GRAND MASTER

- CocoTutti Chocolates
- Michael's Chocolates
- Panache Chocolatier
- Tandem Chocolates

FIVE STAR AWARDS

MASTER CHOCOLATIER

- Banyan Tree Chocolate
- Calgary ChocoSweeats Factorie
- EHChocolatier
- For Pete's Sake Chocolate
- Hot Chocolat
- Moser Roth Chocolate
- SELEUSS Chocolates
- Wildwood Chocolate

FOUR STAR AWARDS

SUPERIOR CHOCOLATIER

- 17 Rocks Pty Ltd
- 3D Candies
- Baetz Chocolates
- Crack'd Toffee Company
- Delysia Chocolatier
- DGZ Chocolates / TOFFARAZZI
- Dolce Lusso Confections
- Echo Chocolate
- Endorfin Foods
- Goufrais
- Hazelnut Hill
- Holm Made Toffee Co. LLC
- Honduras Chocolate Company
- Jonboy Caramels
- PLAYin CHOC
- Tennessee Toffee Co.
- The Confectionist
- Tomo Toffee
- Treat Dreams

THREE STAR AWARDS

EXCEPTIONAL CHOCOLATIER

- Amano Artisan Chocolate
- Bella Sophia Chocolates
- Craft-Chocolate
- Fort Worth Fudge and Toffee, LLC
- Fritz Toffee Company
- Good Good Chocolates
- Hu Chocolate
- Kindred Cooks Caramels
- Kwoka Caramel
- Mashpi Chocolate
- Rainy Day Chocolate
- St. Croix Chocolate Co.
- Sweet Jules Gifts Farm
- Sweet Mona's
- The Oakland Chocolate Company
- Toni's Toffee

COLLECTING LIFESTYLE BOOKS

Recommended Culinary and Home Design
Books for Your Reference Library

"Eat California: Vibrant Recipes From The West Coast" by Vivian Lui, published by Smith Street Books

"Taste of Tucson: Sonoran-Style Recipes Inspired by the Rich Culture of Southern Arizona" by Jackie Alpers, published by West Margin Press

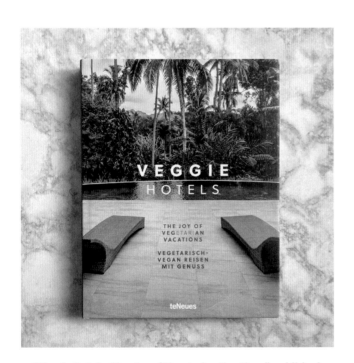

"Veggie Hotels: The Joy of Vegetarian Vacations" published by teNeues

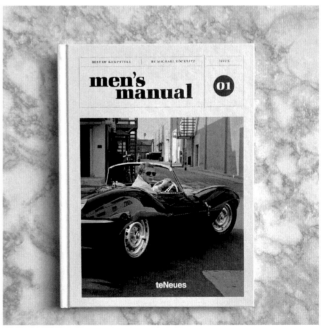

"Men's Manual: Best of Rampstyle" by Michael Kockritz, published teNeues

"The Stylish Life: Yachting" by Kim Kavin, published by teNeues

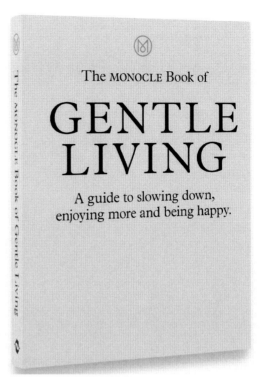

"The Monocle Guide to Gentle Living: A Guide to Slowing Down, Enjoying More and Being Happy" by Tyler Brulé, published by Thames & Hudson

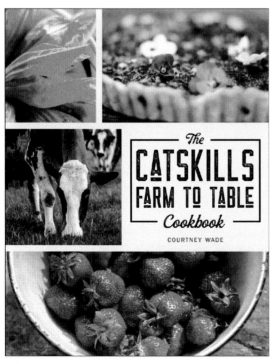

"The Catskills Farm to Table Cookbook" by Courtney Wade, published by Hatherleigh Press

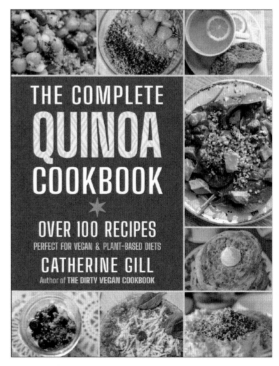

"The Complete Quinoa Cookbook: Over 100 Recipes - Perfect for Vegan & Plant-Based Diets" by Catherine Gill, published by Hatherleigh Press

WORLD DOG SURFING CHAMPIONSHIPS GIFT GUIDE

The World Championships for Dog Surfing take place on the Northern California coast -- where the concept for the dog surfing sport originated -- bringing together the best in local and international dog surfing talent. The world's top dog surfers as well as amateurs are invited to bring home the gold.

Here are some Surf Dog picks for the champions in your life!

WDSC SWEATSHIRT: SURF DOG ON WAVE PORTRAIT #1
This live shot of an awesome surf dog has been recreated as a piece of watercolor art, on a warm and snug 50% cotton sweatshirt. Show you have taste in dogs, cool sports, and modern art. On Your Chest!
http://www.surfdogchampionships.com/shop/

DERBY CALIFORNIA HOODIES
World Dog Surfing Champs Derby & California are not only appearing now in Amazon Prime's new series, The Pack, they also have a new line of groovy hoodies and t-shirts. Be part of their fan pawparazzi!
https://derbycalifornia.com/

A WDSC SURF PACK T-SHIRT
Speaking of Packs, you can form your own when wearing this WDSC Surf Pack long-sleeve t-shirt. You can call your pack whatever you want, BTW. Just not "Sam"
http://www.surfdogchampionships.com/shop/

PET RENU SHAMPOO FOR CLEAN DOGS
Keep your (or a friend's) pup clean, fresh, and flea free with this line of dog shampoos from Pet Renu. A clean dog is a happy dog (owner).
https://www.petrenu.com/Default.asp

FUN PET SERVICES AT WAG HOTELS
Wag Hotels is a great place to board your pet while on a trip away, but even if you stay in town it's also great for daycare, training, and even stylish grooming. Makes a nice gift certificate for next year too.
http://www.waghotels.com

HANKS DOG STUFF POOP TRANSPORTER
Because when "someone's got to go" someone else has to clean it up.
At least look stylish and prepared while doing it.

KEEP THEM DRY AND WARM IN A STUNT PUPPY JACKET
In the winter it's colder and usually wetter… even if you have fur. Stunt Puppy jackets will take care of that problem for the dog in your life. And, they look pretty cool too.

PET CBD FROM VETCBD
If your dog or cat has any issues like these then VETCBD can:
- Support joint mobility

- Support normal brain function
- Help maintain normal GI health
- Help promote calmness

BTW, not officially tested on humans, in case you have any bright ideas.
https://vetcbd.com/

URBAN DENIM LOUNGE BED FROM PET P.L.A.Y.
You might want to curl up on this lounge bed yourself, but you'll just have to stay on your sad old couch. Lead-free zippers for chewers, Eco-friendly all around, and machine washable.

TASTY DOG-THEMED WINE FROM MUTT LYNCH WINERY
A long-time partner of the WDSC, Muttlynch is based in Sonoma County, and you know what that means. Yup, It means that their wine is delicious. Also, all of their bottles have dogs on them.
www.Muttlynchwinery.com

A COLD BOTTLE OF ALE FROM PEDRO POINT BREWING
OK, maybe it's not just Ale. It's "Ale-armingly" good! LOL
They also have Pilsners, IPAs, and Sour and Fruit beers too. And they LOVE dogs

A HIP NEW COLLAR FROM DOOG
What self-respecting pooch wants to wear the collar you have on them now? The answer, none! Or maybe, let's say, a very small number. DOOG has collars that your friends will stop you and say, "Dude, where did you get that cool collar, and why didn't you get me one for the Holidays?" And you'll be like, "Dude, I did!"

DOG FOOD AT PET FOOD EXPRESS
Because a dog's gotta eat, so you might as well make it the best "eatings" they can get, from a wide selection and with the help of a knowledgeable and friendly staff. They can also give that pup a good Holiday wash and trim, now or in next year.

A DOG BANDANA FROM CALIFORNIA CANINE

You know the old saying, "If you really love someone, you'll give them a cool dog bandana." So, how much love do you have? That bandana needs to be on someone special's gift list. BTW, California Canine has other cool accessories too.
https://california-canine.com/

WORLD DOG SURFING CHAMPIONSHIPS V2 COTTON CAP
We guarantee, you wear this hat, people will talk to you. Or at least give you great service. And a smile. In this year, that's a lot.
http://www.surfdogchampionships.com/shop/

THE GOUGHNUTS DOG TOY, YOU CAN THROW IT AND THEY CAN CHEW IT. EVERYONE IS HAPPY
You throw, they bring it back, then they chew on it. Maybe they don't even bring it back, maybe they just sit down and have a good gnaw. A very good, happy, healthy, satisfying gnaw. That's what a dog really wants. You can tell, this gift idea is just gnawing at you
https://www.goughnuts.com/

SUPPORT ROCKET DOG RESCUE
A nice donation or adoption goes a long way to changing a life.
https://www.rocketdogrescue.org/

SUPPORT PENINSULA HUMANE SOCIETY
Saying it twice, because it's still true.
A nice donation or adoption goes a long way to changing a life.
https://phs-spca.org/

GOT TASTE?

EXPERIENCE TasteTV

FOOD ▪ WINE ▪ LIFESTYLE ▪ DESIGN ▪ CHOCOLATE

TasteTV Host
Susan Jones

www.TasteTV.com